RECRUITING 101

The Fundamentals of Being a Great Recruiter

STEVEN MOSTYN, MBA

REVIEWS

"Anyone passionate about recruitment and talent acquisition and looking for training and information on how to be successful must read this book by Steven."
Allan Gosyne, Director of Talent Management at Collins Recruitment Group

"This is a must read for all recruiters or anyone interested in the recruitment field. Steven provides no-nonsense, pragmatic advice and Best Practices that work in today's talent-driven marketplace. His passion for recruitment is both motivating and contagious!"
David Szary, founder of Lean Human Capital & the Recruiter Academy

"For anyone looking to learn the ins and outs of recruitment, look no further! Steven's in-depth, yet easy to understand, analysis of recruitment will provide anyone the building blocks to succeed in the world of recruitment. This book is an essential tool for anyone who wants to learn the basics of recruitment or wants to take their skills to the next level."
Jacob T. Cook, Campus Recruiter, Florida Hospital

"Recruiting 101: Fifteen Fundamentals to Being a Great Recruiter is simple and straight to the point. It will be an invaluable tool to any recruiter starting out in the industry or someone looking to brush up on their skills."
Jeff Chaitoff, CEO, Coastal Staffing Solutions

"Steven Mostyn is no doubt the most talented individual that I know in the field of candidate sourcing. Having been in the Talent Acquisition/Human Resources field for over 30 years, I

can confidently say that Steven is an expert who is tremendously respected in his field."
Korinne Carpino, HR Director, Talent Acquisition, Adventist Health System

"Steven is one of the top sourcing and recruiting experts in the world. Read this book to tap into Steven's vast professional knowledge of recruiting."
Lee Callison, Director of Recruitment, C & C Personnel, LLC

"Although some may think that the methodology that Steven shares is common sense, they would be missing the point. It's the consistent application of tried-and-true methods that bring success, that and being open to staying current with technology and tools—something Steven has always done."
Liza Voticky, Group Director, Talent Acquisition North America, The Coca-Cola Company

"Finally, a book on recruiting that isn't formulaic! Mr. Mostyn outlines implementing success in a visual and anecdotal manner, engaging both recruiting professionals and novices. His section on texting proves he is progressive in his techniques and shares insight anyone who is looking for talent can use, be it a hiring manager or a CEO. As a working mother and global recruiting manager, I learned a lot quickly because it's a fun and fast read!"
Nicole Ilynn Nespeca, Multilingual, Global Sourcing Talent Acquisition Leader, MSC Industrial Direct

"Steven Mostyn is transforming the standard sourcing practice in the talent acquisition industry. His extraordinary speed in communication and readiness to make change inspires all who surround him to act. Steven constantly remains in learning mode, enabling him to be current in the latest technologies and the most relevant data points, ultimately driving value back to his team and colleagues."
Nikki Kemp, eSourcing and Strategic Recruitment Manager, Adventist Health System

"Steven is a true sourcing guru; he knows 1001 ways to find and contact candidates."
Olga Larionova, Senior Sourcing Consultant, PeopleScout

"Steven is a guru in sourcing the most complex profiles and is the ultimate subject matter expert in recruiting/hiring organization design, recruiting operations, and recruiting best practice. I highly recommend this book for someone who wants to learn the art of full cycle Talent Management."
Rene Elhadad, Senior Corporate Talent Management Advisor

"I have known Steve for well over decade now and consider him to be a leading recruiting and sourcing expert. I have witnessed Steve mentor and coach others, sharing his deep recruiting knowledge and expertise. I encourage anyone looking to learn recruitment fundamentals to solicit help from Steve and pick up his book."
Robert Navarrete, Head of Talent Acquisition, Canada at SAS

"Steven is one of the best leaders and mentors a new recruiter could have. He is an expert in data mining, Boolean logic and internet sourcing. He is patient and willing to share his knowledge and experiences. He can relate to candidates at all levels and is capable of finding qualified talent using old school and new methods. He is one of the most sought-after experts by leadership and peers for advice and encouraging outside-the-box thinking to fill niche roles."
Sonja Gay, Americas Sourcer, Willis Towers Watson

"Steven Mostyn is able to share his knowledge, expertise, and experience in recruitment and sourcing and make it directly relatable to the issues and challenges of finding top talent that organizations face today. Readers will better understand how these specific competencies drive individual effectiveness to positively impact their business."
Steven Walesch, Associate Director Talent Acquisition, Florida Hospital

"Steven Mostyn is one of the top sourcing & recruiting experts, and I would recommend this book to any recruiter who wants to learn how to be a great recruiter. I have been in the recruiting industry for 20 years and have not come across anyone more knowledgeable or professional in regards to sourcing and recruiting."
Tim Lawlor, Manager, Recruiting at Yoush Consulting

RECRUITING 101
The Fundamentals of Being a Great Recruiter

STEVEN MOSTYN, MBA

Copyright © 2016 by Steven Mostyn

All rights reserved.

This book contains material protected under International and Federal Copyright Laws and Treaties. No part of this book may be reproduced in any form or by any electronic or mechanical means, including information storage and retrieval systems, without permission in writing from the author. The only permissible exception is for reviewers, who may quote short excerpts in a review.

Terms and Conditions:

The purchaser of this book is subject to the condition that he/she shall in no way resell it, nor any part of it, nor make copies of it for distribution.

The information contained within is strictly for educational purposes only. If you wish to apply ideas contained in this book, you are taking full responsibility for your actions. Accordingly, the author and publisher make no guarantee or warranties as to the accuracy, adequacy or completeness of the results to be obtained from using the work, including any information that can be accessed through the work via hyperlink or otherwise, and expressly disclaim any warranty, express or implied, including but not limited to implied warranties of merchantability or fitness for a particular purpose. The author and publisher do not warrant or guarantee that the function contained in the work will meet your requirements or that its operation will be uninterrupted or error free. Neither the author nor publisher shall be liable to you or anyone else for any inaccuracy, error or omission, regardless of cause, in the work or for any damages resulting therefrom. The author and publisher have no responsibility for the content of any information accessed through the work. Under no circumstances shall the author or publisher be liable for any indirect, incidental, special, punitive, consequential or similar damages that result from the use of or inability to use the work, even if any of them have been advised of the possibility of such damages. This limitation of liability shall apply to any claim or cause whatsoever whether such claim arises in contract, tort or otherwise.

Recruiting 101: The Fundamentals of Being a Great Recruiter
First Edition: 2016
ISBN-13: 978-0991490028
ISBN-10: 0991490029

This book is dedicated to my wife Sarah.

Thank you for being the most caring, supportive
and wonderful wife anyone could ever wish for.
All my achievements are through your merits.
With all my love, I thank you.

CONTENTS

PREFACE

By opening this book, you have taken the first step in your quest to advance your recruitment skills.

Although *Recruiting 101* is intended primarily for the junior/intermediate recruiter, all can benefit from it—from the beginner to the most advanced practitioner. This book is your step-by-step guide to developing the essential skills needed to be successful in this challenging and competitive field.

Why is this book needed?

In my years of experience managing and training recruiters and sourcers, I have met countless recruiters who lacked the basic skills needed to be a successful professional. Without a working knowledge of the core recruitment skills and thereby unable to master the basics, the best efforts of many recruiters are stymied. The result? Failure and frustration.

Seeing the need to educate the wider recruitment audience, I have written this comprehensive recruitment and sourcing guide to enable recruiters to develop these essential foundation skills and take their careers to the next level.

Recruiting 101 was written with the busy recruiting professional in mind: the writing is clear, the format is simple, the chapters are brief and straightforward. Each of the 15 essential skills has its own chapter, making them easy to find and use as reference points. To get the most out of this guide, read it more than once. Apply what you learn. When you reach the end, you will have a good foundation of skills to build a strong recruiting career upon.

Read on, and start your journey to success.

15 FUNDAMENTALS TO BEING A GREAT RECRUITER

Through years of recruiting and sourcing, I have determined there are 15 fundamental skills required to be successful as a recruiter. Below you will find an outline of these fifteen skills, each of which corresponds with a section in this book. By learning and applying these fundamental skills, you will become a great recruiter.

1. Keep motivated, maintain a positive attitude and never give up.
2. Develop strong relationships with your hiring managers.
3. Always conduct detailed intake sessions.
4. Bulk up your domain knowledge: understand your industry, know your organization or client, and know the positions you recruit for inside and out.
5. Employ cutting-edge recruitment marketing: create effective job postings; utilize search engine optimization, branding, social media; post on paid

job boards, free job postings & aggregators.

6. Create your own personal recruitment brand.
7. Use innovative techniques to source your candidates: improve ROT; search using social media, Boolean searches, ATS/CRMs, paid resume databases, open web sourcing; connect using advanced networking.
8. Become a master in the art of cold calling.
9. Know your candidates and keep up to date on trending candidate habits.
10. Interview & select candidates.
11. Sell your organization and hiring managers on the fast hiring process.
12. Improve your closing technique.
13. Give your clients and candidates exceptional customer service.
14. Use data analytics to improve results.
15. Never stop learning.

1:
MOTIVATION, POSITIVE ATTITUDE AND THE FORTITUDE TO NEVER GIVE UP

In any pursuit, an individual will face multiple obstacles and failures. Often, the difference between success and failure is that, despite obstacles, a successful person never gives up.

To truly be successful, an individual has to taste some form of failure and move on to greater heights. Many recruiters leave the industry after a very short period of time because they give up after experiencing failure.

In any discipline there are going to be many ups and downs. Recruitment is no different. One month you are a star with many hires; at other times, despite all of your efforts, you have things that go wrong and you feel like a chump. To truly be successful in any pursuit, you must have the fortitude to never to give up in the face of adversity.

WHAT DO THE FOLLOWING 10 FAMOUS INDIVIDUALS HAVE IN COMMON?

1. Abraham Lincoln
2. Albert Einstein
3. Dr. Seuss
4. J.K. Rowling
5. Michael Jordan
6. Oprah Winfrey
7. Steve Jobs
8. Sylvester Stallone
9. Walt Disney
10. Winston Churchill

Although they were all rejected in pursuit of their dreams, they never gave up and became number one in their professions!

Abraham Lincoln had a multitude of failures in his life, including losing major elections, failing in business, and having a nervous breakdown. Despite these setbacks, Lincoln went on to become one of the greatest presidents in the history of the United States of America.

Albert Einstein did not speak until he was 3 years old, and he was told by his teachers that he would never amount to anything. Einstein is now considered one of the greatest physicists who ever lived.

Dr. Seuss was rejected 27 times before publishing his first book. Today he is considered one of the most beloved children's authors of all time.

J.K. Rowling was dirt poor and was rejected by many publishers before getting her first Harry Potter novel published. The book is now one of the highest-selling of all time.

Michael Jordan was cut from his high school basketball team, but is now widely considered to be the greatest basketball player ever.

Oprah Winfrey was fired from one of her first news anchor jobs after being deemed a bad fit for television. She went on to become one of the most famous television hosts of all time.

Steve Jobs was fired from his own company and considered finished. He made a huge comeback and was rehired by Apple, helping transform the company into one of the most successful businesses in the world.

Sylvester Stallone was poor and struggled as an actor before writing and starring in Rocky. He ended up winning an Oscar and starred in many other blockbuster films.

Walt Disney was fired from his newspaper job for having a lack of imagination. He went on to create the Disney company, one of the most beloved animation studios of all time.

Winston Churchill is considered one of the greatest wartime leaders ever and a World War II hero. Prior to this success, Churchill failed so badly during World War I that he was dismissed from his political party for incompetence.

MY OWN STORY

My parents were told by my second grade teacher that I would never amount to anything due to my extreme hyperactivity. Despite my early academic challenges, I wound up winning a scholarship for my undergraduate degree and obtained my MBA with a perfect 4.0 grade point average.

In my recruitment career, I have also had many struggles.

At my first recruitment job, I was told by the vice president of recruitment that the managers made a mistake by hiring me. He said I did not have the right personality to be a successful recruiter. Instead of taking the VP's words to heart, I was motivated to work harder. I wound up being the top rookie recruiter at my first job, while soon afterward, the VP who said I would not make it was out of the recruitment business.

In addition, at my first corporate recruitment leadership job, the senior VP told me she wanted to fire me in my first week due to my unique and progressive recruitment style. After I produced exceptional results, she became one of my biggest supporters.

Never accept failure and don't take criticism to heart. Instead of being frustrated and downtrodden with failures, use these setbacks to motivate yourself to move forward.

HOW DO YOU STAY POSITIVE?

The following 10 recommendations are great ways for Recruiters to keep positive:

1. Dwell on the positive and not the negative. Every day, list all of the positive things you have done.
2. Try to only associate with positive people. Negative people only bring you down, so keep to the company of positive people.
3. Read inspirational books, quotes, articles and watch inspirational movies.
4. Think of mistakes as learning experiences. Don't dwell on them.

5. Keep track of your successes, and whenever you feel down, take a look at your successes as a reminder of what you have done.
6. Whenever you have negative thoughts, have a mentor or friend you trust motivate you out of your negative thoughts.
7. Learn how to accept and adapt to change. In life, there are many things outside of our control. What we can't control we have to accept.
8. Do not take failure and criticism to heart. Move on from being a victim to a survivor who triumphs over adversity.
9. Focus on what you currently have, not on what you do not have.
10. Visualize a positive future and all of the possibilities that are endless.

YOU OWE IT TO YOURSELF TO NEVER GIVE UP!

Recruitment has its ups and downs. It is easy to be upbeat when things are going right. When things go wrong, it can be a real test of your fortitude.

Recruitment is a business of people and not furniture. That being the case, anything can go wrong because people are unpredictable. On any given day, the unexpected can happen: candidates not accepting offers, candidates who don't show for interviews, and hiring managers taking their frustrations out on you. No matter what happens, always remember that these are just temporary setbacks.

You owe it to yourself to not give up on your career despite setbacks. Any negative situation that arises is just temporary. You can overcome anything as long as you never give up.

2:
RELATIONSHIP
MANAGEMENT

One of the most overlooked skills in recruitment is relationship management. In order to be successful in your recruitment role, you need to develop effective relationships with your hiring managers.

Without a developed relationship with your hiring managers, a recruiter will never be truly successful—regardless of their level of skill in attracting top candidates.

FIRST STEP: RESEARCH YOUR HIRING MANAGER

It is recommended that when you are first assigned to a new hiring manager, you do in-depth research on your new hiring manager. Having some pre-history will better prepare you to understand how to serve the needs of that manager.

The first step you should take is to look them up on LinkedIn and learn about their overall background and work history.

From there, ask other recruiters, HR/recruitment leaders, and other hiring managers about that hiring manager. Below are some questions you should ask in your research:

1. Is this person easy to work with?
2. Is this person generally picky in his or her hiring decisions?
3. What is the best form of communication with this manager?
4. What are some of the hiring manager's pet peeves?
5. What are some of the hiring manager's interests, such as sports, family, and traveling? (You will use this information later during your introduction.)
6. How responsive is this hiring manager when submitting candidates?
7. Does the hiring manager make quick offers?

Finally, look up past requisitions (reqs) to learn what roles the hiring manager has needed in the past. This information will tell you what roles were open, how long they were open, and other information to help you better understand the hiring manager.

HOW TO INTRODUCE YOURSELF

It is recommended that you make your first introduction by phone. Calling will give you a more personable touch than email or texting. Contacting by email or text should only be used if calling is not possible.

During this first conversation, briefly explain to the hiring manager who you are and that you have been assigned to work with him or her.

Tell the hiring manager you look forward to building this relationship and would like to schedule a face-to-face meeting. Also emphasize that an in-person meeting will help you better understand the company's staffing needs and help fill their roles. Assure the manager that your goal is not just to fill roles but to provide excellent customer service.

Most hiring managers will see value in this meeting and respect your extra level of customer service.

Try to schedule the meeting as soon as you can so that it will be fresh on the hiring manager's radar.

FIRST MEETING WITH THE HIRING MANAGER

If possible, your first meeting with the hiring manager should be in person to solidify your relationship. This will increase the trust level, and you will be more than just a voice on the phone.

Start the conversation positively by telling the hiring manager how much you look forward to helping with the company's staffing needs. From there, give the hiring manager a brief bio of yourself.

Even if you are not the most experienced recruiter, you should make the hiring manager feel at ease by exuding confidence through your speech and demeanor.

After your introductions are completed, you should let the

hiring manager do most of the talking. You want to learn as much as possible about them and the department.

During this meeting, you should use all the market intelligence you gathered about the hiring manager to establish your knowledge and ability. This is when you bring up the interests of the hiring manager (that you found during your research) to build rapport.

DEVELOPING TRUST WITH YOUR HIRING MANAGER

For most hiring managers, trust is something that must be earned; it is not automatically given. Trust will be earned in small increments by every positive thing you do for your hiring manager. Below are ways you can earn points with your hiring manager and develop trust:

1. **Get hires.** This is the most obvious way to develop trust with your hiring manager. If they see you can deliver, they will begin to trust you.
2. **Submitting the right candidates.** Showing that you listened and understood the company's needs during intake by submitting the right candidates provides lots of creditability in hiring managers' books.
3. **Do not delay contacting candidates.** Hiring managers hate when candidates are not contacted quickly.
4. **Make quick offers.** Nothing will tick off a hiring manager more than delaying or losing a candidate at

the offer stage.

5. **Be honest.** Hiring managers would rather you be honest with them than blow smoke about something you do not know or cannot do.

6. **Provide exceptional customer service.** Perception is everything—you can get tons of hires and still have no trust with your hiring manager. If the hiring manager perceives you as not providing good service, they will not trust you.

7. **Always return your manager's calls, texts, and emails.** Managers want to feel important. Therefore, without exception, always return your hiring manager's phone calls, emails and texts as soon as you can.

8. **Always be available for your manager via many forms of communication—phone, email, text and instant messenger.** By making yourself available via more than one form of communication, you will earn credibility with your hiring manager.

9. **Go the extra mile for your hiring managers.** Sometimes going the extra mile can go a long way. For example, an extra thing you can do for your hiring manager is to give them market intelligence.

10. **After making hires, send thank-you emails.** After your candidates get hired by your hiring manager, send a thank-you note to the hiring manager expressing your appreciation for their partnership.

11. **Under-promise and over-deliver.** Never promise something you cannot deliver. Instead, over-deliver and your hiring manager will be eating out of your hand.

HOW TO IMPROVE A SHATTERED RELATIONSHIP WITH YOUR HIRING MANAGER

A shattered relationship with your hiring manager should be a major concern, and must be healed in order to move forward with business. There are many reasons why relationships get shattered. Below are some of those reasons, followed by solutions on how to repair them:

1. **Inheriting a hiring manager who has a tempestuous relationship with your colleague.**

    There could be many reasons why a relationship between your colleague and hiring manager fail. Your first step is to do research and find out what caused the break in the relationship. Once you know the cause, you can move forward to resolve the issue.

    During your first phone call, do everything you can to make the hiring manager feel at ease. Explain that you are a different recruiter, and that you would like the opportunity to provide a level of service they did not receive with the previous recruiter.

    It is paramount in this type of relationship that you go the extra mile and follow the previous eleven ways to develop trust with a hiring manager. Over time, the hiring manager will trust you and you can move forward with business.

2. **Not able to deliver a hire, or even a slate of candidates.**

    At times, even top-of-the-food-chain recruiters are unable to fill a certain role or find suitable candidates.

Even if the role is unfillable, some hiring managers might consider you a failure and not want to continue to work with you. In this case, your best bet is to put your consulting shoes on and make the hiring manager feel at ease. Assure them that you will continue to deliver for them. Give them examples of your past successes to remind them you consistently deliver.

Another option is to provide data to the hiring manager about the realities of the market and the reason why the role is unfillable. A great tool I recommend using in this case is Wanted Analytics, which can provide recent data about the supply and demand of the role locally and the difficulty to fill that role. This tool will be further explained in Chapter 14.

After giving the hiring manager the realities of the market, provide suggestions on alternative ways to fill the role. Some suggestions include alterative profiles and relocating candidates.

3. **Hiring manager with misconstrued ideas about your performance.**

Again, perception is everything and unfortunately there can be times when a hiring manager has the wrong perception about you. Examples include: thinking you do not have their best interests at heart, you are not trying your best, or other misconstrued ideas about your performance. In this case, you have to be straightforward with the hiring manager to address the misconception. After you find the root cause of this misconception, do everything you can to make the hiring manager feel you are working in the manager's best interests and demonstrate by your actions that the misconception is not true.

SOME RELATIONSHIPS ARE NOT WORTH KEEPING

Just like in your personal life, there are relationships that are worth keeping and those you should end. In recruitment, there are times when no matter what you do, a specific hiring manager and you will not be a match. When this occurs, it is recommended that you switch out and move on to another hiring manager and let one of your colleagues take over. This should be a worst-case scenario. But in some circumstances, you will avoid even more acrimony by ending the relationship. This will allow you to move on to a better situation where you can once again be successful in your hiring manager relationships.

3:
INTAKE SESSIONS

Intake sessions are detailed meetings you have with your hiring managers in which you learn all of the important information about the requisition you have received. These sessions are essential to understanding the true needs of your external and internal clients.

THE IMPORTANCE OF INTAKE SESSIONS

Would a contractor build a custom house for a client without blueprints? The end product would not be the client's custom house, but the builder's own design. This is basically what happens when a recruiter does not conduct an intake session. This is a recipe for failure. In essence, an intake session is where a recruiter gets the verbal blueprints from the hiring manager. Without this information, a recruiter will most likely fail in filling the assigned role for their client.

Think about a customer in a restaurant who orders a hamburger but gets a hotdog instead. This is what happens when recruiters do not do a proper intake. They end up with the wrong profile for their hiring managers.

Without a good intake session, recruiters will base their search solely on the job description. This can result in setting qualifications too high or too low instead of the true profile the hiring managers expect and deserve.

WORKING WITHOUT A PROPER INTAKE SESSION WASTES TIME

Two of the biggest fundamentals of recruiting is time and accuracy. You will learn more about the importance of time in Chapter 7, which focuses on sourcing. The reason many recruiters do not successfully deliver candidates to their hiring managers is that they did not do a proper intake session. By not taking the time in the beginning of the search to speak to a hiring manager and conduct a proper intake, the recruiter will end up wasting a lot of time and effort searching for a candidate based on an inaccurate profile that does not reflect the hiring manager's needs.

By having a proper intake session with your hiring manager, you can avoid hours of frustration that often result in a list of candidates ill-suited to the role you're trying to fill.

THE ART OF A GOOD INTAKE SESSION

If you were playing basketball and had the option of lowering the basket for every shot so you could win, would you do it?

When a recruiter does not ask the right questions during an intake session, they are, in effect, raising the basket instead of lowering it. They are making the goal harder to reach and the results end up being the opposite of what they intended. If the hiring manager is not probed during an intake session, he or she will most likely not provide key information that will make finding qualified candidates easier. By simply learning the art of a good intake session, recruiters will be able to ask the right questions and create a profile that results in a focused and productive search.

Another key misstep recruiters make is having short intake sessions in order to save time. This is a mistake because detailed intakes will allow the recruiter to obtain all of the information they need to fill their roles.

QUESTIONS TO ASK DURING THE INTAKE SESSION

Following are 30 questions you should ask your hiring manager during an intake session. Getting these key questions answered can make your search much easier and effectively help you find the right slate of candidates for your hiring manager.

1. **What is the true profile the hiring manager is seeking?** Tell the hiring manager that you want to go beyond a job description, and for them to take their time and determine the exact person they are looking for with all the qualifications. Asking for those key

qualifications will help you find the right talent.

2. **Is the hiring manager willing to look at alternative candidates?** You never know unless you ask! Many hiring managers will take alterative profiles. For example, many hospitals will take PCU nurses for an ICU job opening. In the technology sector, some clients will take senior developers who have done enterprise design as software architects. There are many more examples, so do not be afraid to ask!

3. **Does the hiring manager have any internal or external candidates in mind?** This is very important because the hiring manager might already have an internal or external candidate identified for the role. If you were to source for this position, you would be wasting your time.

4. **What salary is the hiring manager willing to offer?** When asking about salary, it never hurts to ask the hiring manager if they are willing to exceed the salary range for the right candidate. Many hiring managers will pay extra for hard-to-fill jobs if you bring them top talent.

5. **Is the salary is on par with current market rates?** This will tell you how hard the role will be to fill based on the compensation being too low or high compared to the market.

6. **How many years of experience in the domain do the candidates need?** Would the manager consider a candidate with less experience? How many years? Many times, job descriptions are generic and ask for specific years of experience, but the hiring manager might be open to a candidate with less experience. This, in turn, could open up the market for you.

7. **What type of person fits into the department?** Find out about the people already working in the department. Are they easygoing? Type A? Knowing this will help you find candidates who will fit into the department, get hired, and not leave after short stints.

8. **What are the benefits of working for the department and organization?** Find out why someone would want to work for the organization and department. Has the company or department ever won awards? Are they using state-of-the-art equipment? Are they innovative? Is it a brand new department? Is there stability in both the organization and the department?

9. **Other than salary, what are other tangible benefits of the job?** Does the job have a bonus? How is it earned and how much is it? Is there a sign-on bonus and, if so, how much? Would management consider a sign-on bonus for hard-to-fill roles? What are the health care benefit costs? Many parents need day care, so ask if there is a subsidized day care. Is there a stock option? For start-ups, this will be a great benefit. Is there a retirement plan or 401k? Is there a fitness membership offered? What is the vacation policy? Is there flexibility, with extra days that can be negotiated? Can the role be virtual or have flexible hours? Ask for any other tangible benefits—you will be surprised what some organizations will offer. A great example is Netflix's offering one year of paid maternal/paternal leave for employees who are new parents.

10. **What does the typical day look like?** Ask the hiring manager to give information on what a typical day in the life of the incumbent looks like.

11. **Are there promotional opportunities?** What does the opportunity for advancement look like? What would be the most logical next step after this role?

12. **What is the hiring manager's management style?** You can use this information to either sell candidates on good managers or determine which candidates might clash with a particular hiring manager.

13. **Who are the competitors?** The competition is often the best place to recruit.

14. **Where have they found candidates in the past?** Ask what organizations the hiring manager has successfully hired from in the past. This can show you great places focus your efforts.

15. **What profiles or candidates from specific organizations have not been successful fits in the past?** This can tell you possible places where candidates may not be a fit. This, in turn, can save you time recruiting candidates from this type of organization.

16. **How long have similar roles been open in the past?** This will tell you how difficult filling the role might be.

17. **How long has the role been open?** The answer to this question will give you an indication of how difficult filling it will be.

18. **Why is the role open?** Is it a back-fill or a result of growth in the department? This information will tell you a lot about the state of the company.

19. **What does the department currently look like?** If the retention is good, it means the department is most likely a good place to work. Alternatively, if retention is not good, that is a red flag for problems

in the department.

20. **What are the nice-to-haves for the role?** This information can help you find the most attractive candidates.

21. **Would the company consider relocating a candidate?** If yes, would they pay for relocation? To expand the search, find out if the hiring manager would be interested at looking at profiles of candidates outside the local area. If they will pay for relocation, what does that package look like?

22. **Would you sponsor a candidate from another country?** For rare skill sets, the domestic market might not have the candidate pool necessary to land the right talent. Ask the hiring manager if the company will sponsor candidates from other countries.

23. **What education and certifications do the candidates need?** Ask if there is any flexibility on these requirements. Having some flexibility will open up the candidate pool.

24. **What individuals outside of their organization would a hiring manager recommend for this role?** This question can make recruiting for the role easy, as it will provide a list of individuals to contact who the hiring manager is already is interested in.

25. **If the role is at a management level, how many direct reports will the candidate have?** This is important as most leaders want to know the size of the team they are going to manage.

26. **Does the role need to be filled quickly?** This will tell you how urgent the hiring manager needs to fill the role. Also, if it is not urgent, you could be wasting

your time on a role the hiring manager may not want to fill right away.

27. **What does the interview process look like?** How many interviews are required? This will let you know what to expect.

28. **Who will do the interviewing?** This will tell you who will be involved in the hiring process.

29. **What are the best days and time of day to schedule interviews?** This will give you an idea of when the hiring manager is available.

30. **Can you schedule interviews directly on the hiring manager's calendar?** This will help you speed up the process.

CONCLUDING THE INTAKE SESSION

After the intake session, give the hiring manager an estimation on long you expect it will take for you to submit candidates as well as what information will be included in that candidate delivery, such as a resume and screening notes.

Very importantly, at the end of the intake, let the hiring manager know that candidates for hard-to-fill roles do not last long in any market, and that your advice to is to move fast on top candidates or be prepared to lose them to competitors. The threat of loss usually pushes a hiring manager to move quickly on candidates.

4:
DOMAIN KNOWLEDGE

- UNDERSTAND YOUR INDUSTRY SPACE
- KNOW YOUR ORGANIZATION OR CLIENT
- KNOW THE POSITIONS YOU RECRUIT INSIDE AND OUT

INTRODUCTION

Domain knowledge is the business intelligence you need to know about the industry you recruit in, your client or organization, and the roles you recruit for. Without this business intelligence, you will not be able to effectively recruit or sell candidates on your client or organization.

Think of a police detective tracking down a suspect and needing clues to be successful. Domain knowledge provides the clues for a recruiter. By having a good understanding of domain knowledge, a recruiter will have the background they need to be successful.

UNDERSTAND YOUR INDUSTRY SPACE

No matter what industry you recruit for, you have to have functional knowledge about that industry to be able to successfully interact with both hiring managers and candidates. This does not mean you have to become a guru in your industry space; it just means you have to be able to have the right conversations. By learning the basics of your industry, and with practice, you will be a pro and be able to have intelligent conversations with hiring managers and candidates.

HOW TO BECOME FUNCTIONALLY INTELLIGENT IN YOUR SPACE

To become functionally intelligent in your space, you need to learn about the industry you recruit in. This can take anywhere from a few weeks in simple spaces like retail to six months in more complicated spaces like technology.

I started recruiting in technology, and it probably took me a good six months to be functionally proficient to the point where I could have detailed conversations with my hiring managers.

In certain spaces, you might become frustrated at first with your lack of knowledge. But with persistence, training and practice, you will become functionally intelligent in your space.

RESEARCH ON YOUR OWN

Start by doing research on your own and learning more about your industry. The obvious best place to start is the web. In Google search, type in the industry you are looking up plus the word "terms." If you are in the technology industry, your search would look like this: "technology terms". Google then brings up a list of sites that can educate you in technology.

Online encyclopedias and Wikipedia are great online places to research your domain industry; there, many terms in your industry can be found as reference points. Finally, the simplest way to search is to type in a word you do not know in the Google browser, and you will get a wealth of answers.

Other than the web, you can research your industry the old-school way by reading books. If you do not have the money to buy books, most public libraries have a wide selection of books at the introductory level.

SPEAK WITH YOUR COLLEAGUES

A great way to learn more about your industry space is to speak to your colleagues. If you come across something technical in your space that you are not familiar with, there is a high probability that your colleagues will know about it. Do not be afraid to ask or sound unintelligent—everybody starts off with no knowledge. Most colleagues have no problems sharing their knowledge when prompted.

TALK TO CANDIDATES

A great way to become proficient in understanding your domain is to speak to candidates. Think of learning a foreign language and practicing with a native speaker. This is true for recruiters learning a new domain. When I was learning aspects of technology years ago, I did not understand terms such as "object-orientated programming languages." By speaking with expert developers, I learned the basics of this subject. Just by speaking with candidates, a recruiter can become proficient in any domain.

KNOW YOUR ORGANIZATION OR CLIENT

It is paramount for recruiters to sell candidates on the organization or the client they represent. The only way to truly sell a candidates on the organization or client is to know all the selling features that the organization or client has to offer.

CREATE A SELLING SHEET

A great way to gather all of the selling features of your organization or client in order to sell candidates is to create a selling sheet.

To create a selling sheet, a recruiter should speak with their hiring managers and colleagues and gather a list of features that can sell the organization or client to candidates. Below are examples of things that can sell candidates on an organization or client:

1. **The stability of the organization** – Many candidates want to work for companies they feel are stable.
2. **The stability of the job** – Candidates like jobs that are stable and not short-term.
3. **Salary of roles** – If the job is paying over market value then salary can be a great selling tool.
4. **Health care benefits** – What kind of health care benefits do they offer? Are the premiums and deductibles low?
5. **Sign-on bonuses** – Do they have roles that offer sign-on bonuses? A sign-on bonus might make the difference in someone signing with the organization.
6. **Yearly bonus** – What kind of yearly bonus is offered?
7. **Stock option and retirement** – Are there stock options or retirement plans offered?
8. **Relocation** – Do they have roles that offer relocation assistance?
9. **Educational reimbursement** – Do they offer educational reimbursement for post-secondary education like MBAs and certifications? How much is offered and what are the conditions?
10. **On-site daycare** – Is there an on-site daycare and what are the rates?
11. **Career growth and advancement** – Is there a proven fast-track for advancement and growth? What does that look like?
12. **The culture of the organization** – A positive place to work is a great selling feature.
13. **Location** – Is the location convenient for commuters? Does the location have something to offer, such as a

warm climate or low cost of living?

14. **Awards** – Awards can sell candidates. Types of awards that sell a company include "best place to work" and industry awards.

15. **Hiring manager** – A nice hiring manager can sell candidates on jobs. Many candidates focus on who they will work for.

16. **Innovations** – A company that is doing something innovative can attract candidates, especially in technology.

17. **Fortune 500** – Many candidates want to work for a large company with a big reputation.

18. **Values** – Many candidates want to work for organizations that are known for strong ethics and values.

19. **New department and start-up** – Some candidates like the challenge of building from scratch, an opportunity that start-ups can offer.

20. **Flexible work schedules** – Offering employees a flexible work schedule can be an important selling feature, especially for parents.

21. **Virtual options** – Offering virtual roles is a huge selling feature.

22. **Maternal and paternity leave** – Offering longer leave for both maternity and paternity is a nice benefit.

23. **Paid time off** – Offering longer paid vacations is a great benefit to sell candidates on.

24. **Free catered food** – Some companies actually provide free catering. For some candidates, having free food is a big selling feature.

25. **Employee health and welfare** – Offering free fitness and wellness is a great perk.

KNOW THE POSITIONS YOU RECRUIT INSIDE AND OUT

When speaking with candidates, if you do not properly understand or can explain the roles you recruit for, you will have a hard time convincing candidates to make a move. Think of a car salesman who doesn't know the make of the car they are selling and can't tell you any of its features. A recruiter who does not properly understand or cannot explain the roles they are trying to fill is not going to be successful.

To land the top candidates, it is vital that you understand these positions inside and out.

When speaking with candidates, you need to be able to paint a picture of the role. You might never be an expert on the role, but you need to be able to understand a role well enough to get a candidate interested.

BEYOND INTAKE SESSIONS

After intake sessions, do not be afraid to ask your hiring manager more questions about the role. Even after the best intake sessions, there can be things you might not understand about a role. Getting extra information about the role might make a difference in selling a candidate on the opportunity.

PRACTICE MAKES PERFECT

When first learning about a role, it might take time to fully grasp its complexities and nuances. This is especially true for technical positions. The more you learn and speak with candidates, the more you will grasp the purpose of the role. You will most likely make mistakes along the way, but practice makes perfect, and over time you will fully understand the role and be able to sell candidates.

DOMAIN KNOWLEDGE CONCLUSION

By understanding the industry you recruit in, your client or organization, and the roles you recruit, you will develop the domain knowledge needed to be successful at your craft.

5: RECRUITMENT MARKETING

- CREATING EFFECTIVE JOB POSTINGS
- SEARCH ENGINE OPTIMIZATION (SEO), RECRUITMENT BRANDING
- SOCIAL MEDIA
- WHY GLASSDOOR MATTERS
- TIPS ON POSTING ON PAID JOB BOARDS
- FREE JOB POSTINGS & AGGREGATORS

Connecting with candidates through recruitment marketing is truly a science, and if done the right way, it can be a tremendous source of candidates for recruiters. On the other hand, recruitment marketing done the wrong way can be an enormous expense, a huge time killer, and worst of all, result in no hires to show for your efforts.

Recruitment Marketing is such an important part of recruitment that in the past decade this specialty has become a whole career offshoot of recruiting.

In this chapter, we will discuss the fundamentals of recruitment marketing, which can increase the flow of candidates, which in turn will help you fill jobs.

CREATING EFFECTIVE JOB POSTINGS

Before recruiters can even focus their efforts on recruitment marketing, they have to have effective job postings.

It is of the upmost importance for recruiters to have good job postings or they will not have good results with marketing.

Many recruiters are simply satisfied with the traditional, archaic method of using a job description they get from hiring managers. Most of these descriptions use generic copy, which in many cases has nothing really to do with the job itself. Also, most of these job descriptions are not search optimized and do not sell candidates on the role or company.

Just to give you some personal insight of the 20-plus high-performing sourcers I currently manage, the highest performers have all mastered the art of creating effective job postings. They have mastered this skill to such a level that many of their hard-to-fill roles get filled simply because they have effective job postings.

In this section, you will learn how to write compelling job descriptions that will sell candidates on the role. In addition, by utilizing search engine optimization (SEO), your roles will be more easily found on the web.

HOW TO WRITE EFFECTIVE JOB TITLES

To start with a good job posting, you need to have an effective job title. Below are some pointers on creating an effective job title:

1. **The job title must be the most common title that is recognizable to external candidates.** For example, if your hiring manager is calling a role something that most candidates will not recognize, you should change it to the most common vernacular. If the hiring manager is calling a role simply "consultant," no one will know what kind of consultant the company is looking for, so the job title should be more specific. If the consultant is actually a project manager role, then the job title should be "project manager" and not "consultant."

2. **Keep your titles as short as possible but with as much searchable information as you can.** From an SEO perspective, long titles are harder to find and clog up SEO algorithms. At the same time, job titles have to be optimized with enough information so that candidates can find the posting on the web.

3. **Be sure to use the word "job" in the job title.** Many people include "job" when looking for a job, so having "job" in the job title will make your jobs more searchable.

4. **Words that are searched together should be placed**

together in the job title. For example, in health care many ICU nurses search for ICU & RN together. Therefore, these words should be placed together in the job title.

5. **Abbreviations should be listed if that is how candidates look up a role.** For example, some accountants look for jobs by typing "CPA" in search box, so "CPA" should be listed in the job title.

6. **Avoid symbols.** Some recruiters use symbols (like *) in job titles when tracking reqs. Symbols are an SEO death sentence in a job title because they affect SEO algorithms. This will prevent your job from being seen by candidates.

7. **Secondary search words are a good idea to add to the job description.** Include a second or third word that a candidate might use to search for a job. For example, in technology some Java developers search by "Java" or "J2EE," so having these secondary words might catch candidates that otherwise would not have seen the job posting.

The following are examples of common job titles in different industries.

1. **Accounting**
   Chartered Accountant - CPA Job

2. **Engineering**
   Mechanical Engineer / Engineering Job

3. **Financial Services**
   Financial Planner / Advisor - CFP Job

4. **Healthcare**
   Registered Nurse Intensive Care Unit/ICU RN Job

5. **Insurance**
   Life Insurance Advisor /Agent Job
6. **Manufacturing**
   Plant Manager / Superintendent Job
7. **Oil & Gas**
   Field Operator / Oil & Gas Job
8. **Pharmaceutical**
   Pharmaceutical Sales Representative/Account
   Manager Job
9. **Retail**
   Retail Store Manager Job
10. **Technology**
    J2EE / Java Developer Job

JOB DESCRIPTIONS SHOULD BEGIN WITH POINTS THAT SELL THE JOB

When looking at job descriptions, candidates have to be sold about a job in the first few sentences. In many cases, these key sentences are wasted with a long-winded description about the organization with little or no selling features.

In order to sell candidates on the job posting, you should ensure your first paragraph is dedicated to selling features of the job. Below are some common selling features that should appear in the first paragraph, preferably with bullet points:

1. Sign-on or relocation bonuses.
2. Awards the organization has won.
3. Career growth and advancement potential.
4. New innovations achieved by the organization.
5. Stock options/retirement plans.

6. Educational reimbursement.
7. On-site discounted daycare.
8. The culture of the organization.
9. Flexible work life balance/virtual office.
10. Other unique and appealing benefits.

Below is an example of how the opening of a good job description should look:

> **Top Reasons why you want to work for Health Hospital as a PCU RN:**
>
> - $10,000 sign-on bonus for qualified candidates.
> - You get to work a minute from the beach.
> - Low cost of living in one of the most affordable parts of Florida.
> - Named a Great Workplace Award winner for the seventh year in a row.
> - Warm weather and outdoor activities 12 months of the year.
> - Career growth and advancement potential.

JOB DESCRIPTIONS THAT ARE ACTUALLY ABOUT THE JOB

One of the most frustrating things is when job descriptions are generic babble and not actually about the job. Most recruiters usually just repost the words provided by their hiring managers. The result is a generic job posting that has nothing to do with the job. Make sure the job description is about the job you are recruiting for!

LONG JOB POSTINGS DO NOT ENGAGE CANDIDATES' ATTENTION

Most candidates today do not have long attention spans. Long job descriptions do not grab their attention. Keep your job posting short and descriptive and you will grab your candidates' attention.

BORING JOB DESCRIPTIONS DO NOT SELL CANDIDATES!

Most recruiters are not professional writers, and many recruiters do not have the luxury of a copywriter. That being the case, it is paramount that recruiters improve the way they write a job description. If you read your own job descriptions and you are bored, it might be time to jazz things up with words that sound more interesting and appealing.

PLACEMENT OF TEXT & FONTS SHOULD BE VISUALLY APPEALING

Also important is the placement of text and use of fonts to attract candidates' attention. Fonts should be large enough and easy to read . At the same time, if they are too large or bold it will be overpowering. The text placement should be centered in such a way that the job description becomes visually appealing.

PUT EEO STATEMENTS AND COMPANY DESCRIPTIONS AT THE END OF THE JOB DESCRIPTION

EEO statements and company descriptions can both be legal and important, but from a candidate's perspective this information will most likely not sell them on a job. Therefore, these items should be placed at the end of a job description.

SEO OF WORD PLACEMENT IS A MUST

We will learn more about SEO in section B. Briefly, SEO word placement is what raises the chances of your job posting appearing high on the list of a candidate's online job search. Examples of SEO are having your title placed throughout your job, listing key words throughout the job, as well as placing them in strategic locations.

PUTTING IT ALL TOGETHER - AN EXAMPLE OF A GREAT JOB DESCRIPTION WHICH IS SEARCH OPTIMIZED

Registered Nurse Progressive Care Unit / PCU RN Job
Company: Health Hospital
Location: Tarpon Springs, Florida

Top Reasons Why You Want to Work for Health Hospital as a PCU RN:

- $10,000 sign-on bonus for qualified candidates.
- You get to work a minute from the beach.
- Low cost of living in one of the most affordable

parts of Florida.

- Named a Great Workplace Award winner for the seventh year in a row.
- Warm weather and outdoor activities 12 months of the year.
- Career growth and advancement potential.

PCU RN Job Responsibilities:

- A progressive care nurse (PCU RN) works in a progressive care unit (PCU) and cares for patients requiring close monitoring but who do not need ICU care.
- PCU RNs monitor cardiac and other vital information and detect any changes, thereby enabling intervention during life-threatening or emergency situations.
- Close observation is necessary as many PCU patients receive a significant amount of complex meds, sometimes through an intravenous line that may need to be adjusted or titrated.
- PCU RNs assess, plan and evaluate patient care needs.
- PCU RNs prioritize patient care based on acuity level and available resources.
- Progressive care registered nurses assist physicians during examination, treatment and procedures.
- PCU RNs administer prescribed medications, change dressings, clean wounds, monitor vital signs.
- PCU RNs may expect to have a nurse/patient ratio of 1:4

Progressive Care Unit Work Hours/Shifts:

- Full Time, Days or Nights

What will you need as a PCU RN / Registered Nurse?

- Florida RN license or the ability to obtain a FL license at the time of start date.
- Basic Life Support (Accredited through American Heart Association or American Red Cross)
- Experience: Minimum 1 year of RN experience is required
- Education: BSN preferred

Registered Nurse Progressive Care Unit / PCU RN Job

This facility is an equal opportunity employer and complies with federal, state and local anti-discrimination laws, regulations and ordinances.

Registered Nurse Progressive Care Unit / PCU RN Job

Registered Nurse, RN, Progressive Care Unit, PCU, Step-Down, Continuous Care, Transitional Care, Tele/Progressive Care/Telemetry, Critical Care, Intermediate Care Units, Direct Observation Units, Step-Down Units, Transitional Care Units, & Progressive Medicine Unit

Tarpon Springs, Clearwater, Dunedin, Palm Harbor, Tampa, Largo, and St. Petersburg.

SEARCH ENGINE OPTIMIZATION (SEO)

Search engine optimization, abbreviated as SEO, is a term for the methods used to increase the number of people who visit a website by obtaining a high-ranking placement in the search results page of a search engine or job board.

There are two types of SEO: 1) Paid; and 2) Organic

WHAT IS PAID SEO?

Organic SEO can be time consuming and can take expertise. That's why some companies are willing to spend money on SEO when posting their jobs. By paying for SEO, companies can achieve search optimization for their jobs.

If paid SEO is done right, organizations can guarantee that their jobs will appear on top of search results.

GOOGLE IS THE KING OF ALL PAID SEO
HTTPS://WWW.GOOGLE.COM/

If you were to survey most job seekers, one of the biggest places they start their job search is Google.

It is true what they say about Google, and that is: if you are not on the first page, you do not exist. Therefore, if you pay Google through their adverting platform called Google AdWords, you can achieve a first-page status.

You can use AdWords either through an ad agency, which can take care of the work for you for a fee, or go at it on your own.

If you decide to go at it alone, things to consider are: setting the price, key words, location, and other key elements you want your targeted ad to cover. Google has minimum prices as well as other restrictions. Google can also be restrictive in terms of ad selection and delivery.

How much you pay will determine where the ad will come up on Google. The final result—if you pay for a Google ad for a Pharmaceutical Sales Representative in Miami Beach, Florida, then consumers who type in those words will find your job on the first page of their search.

OTHER PAID SEO

Other than Google, alternative search engines include Bing, DuckDuckGo and Yahoo. Below you will find a brief summary of each:

1. **Bing** - https://www.bing.com/ Owned by Microsoft, it has a steady flow of users due to Microsoft's penetration of consumers who use Microsoft Internet Explorer browser, which promotes Bing as a search engine.
2. **DuckDuckGo** - https://duckduckgo.com/ This is a fast-growing search engine that some consumers prefer because it protects a searcher's privacy.
3. **Yahoo** - https://www.yahoo.com/ This is one of the oldest search engines with name recognition. Yahoo has a loyal user base and receives traffic through its news and email services.

ORGANIC SEO

Big picture organic recruitment marketing SEO is very important to organizations, as it will allow your jobs to pop up on search engines organically.

As previously mentioned, organic SEO can be time consuming and can take expertise; therefore, some companies either have an internal expert or use an SEO vendor to handle their search optimization.

EASY ORGANIC SEO TIPS FOR YOUR JOB DESCRIPTIONS

An easy way to increase the number of candidates finding your jobs on the web is to improve the SEO of your job descriptions. Doing specific things within your job descriptions will increase its rank in search engines. Below are some key tips to improving the organic SEO of job descriptions, some of which were already mentioned in the job posting section:

1. **Have a relevant job title that most people search for.** Your Job postings will score higher if you use a relevant title that most people search for.
2. **List the actual word "job" in the job title.** Example: ICU Registered Nurse Job. Many people include "job" when looking for a job so having "job" in the job title will make your jobs more searchable.
3. **Avoid symbols in job title.** Some recruiters use symbols (like *) in job titles when tracking reqs. Symbols are an SEO death sentence in a job title, as they effect SEO algorithms. This will prevent your job from being seen by candidates.
4. **List the job title multiple times in the job description.** Strategically placing the job title multiple times in the job description will increase the optimization of the job, and make it rank higher in candidates' searches. The reason is that SEO increases with the number of times key words are placed on a website.
5. **List locations multiple times in the job description as well as other nearby cities that candidates may search.** Listing other locations near your location

might make your job pop up on searches done by job seekers who search by location.

6. **In the skills section, list multiple keywords that candidates may use in a job search.** These terms might be searched by job seekers so having them listed might make your job pop up.

BIG PICTURE ORGANIC SEO TIPS

The following big picture organic SEO tips most likely will be done by internal marketing personnel, but for smaller organizations you might be able to lend a hand. Also, big picture SEO is a field unto itself; therefore, only a few of the major tips are listed:

1. Make sure your website is indexed to all major search engines.
2. Update your website with fresh content. New content scores higher than old content.
3. Link to other websites with similar content.
4. Have similar websites link with your website.
5. Keywords should not be placed randomly on your website. Search engines can lower SEO scores for sites that overdo keywords. Therefore, it is better to hide keywords.
6. You should link to internal pages on your site.
7. Create more content. Content equals more people, which can translate into a higher SEO ranking.

RECRUITMENT BRANDING

Recruitment branding is the art of creating a corporate presence for candidates so that they will recognize your brand, and be interested in becoming employees of that brand.

Most organizations have established recruitment brands, but recruitment could be asked to take part in improving or changing an established brand. As recruitment branding is a topic unto itself, this section will only be an overview. Below you will find some important aspects of recruitment branding:

1. **Define your value proposition.** A brand should have a defined value proposition that will attract candidates.
2. **Build brand awareness.** Building brand awareness is important; it spreads the message. Awareness can be grown by social media, SEO, digital advertising, and traditional media—print, TV, and Radio.
3. **Create brand-centric content.** A recruitment brand can gain followers through building brand-specific content. Positive information centric to the brand should be created to attract followers, which later can be converted into candidates and even hires.
4. **Organizational good deeds.** A great way to grow your brand is through your organization's good deeds. By taking part in acts of charity, your organization can enhance its brand image and gain more followers.
5. **Build talent communities through your brand.** One of the fastest-growing aspects of recruitment branding is building talent communities through your brand. Basically, a talent community is made

up of potential candidates who are interested in your brand and follow your social media and web presence. Through engaging content, these followers are kept and some are converted into hires.

SOCIAL MEDIA

Social media can be a valuable recruitment tool if it is done correctly. The problem for many recruiters is that social media can become more about playing as opposed to actually recruiting talent. This section will show recruiters how to properly use social media from a recruitment perspective.

THE THREE MAIN FUNCTIONS OF SOCIAL MEDIA IN RECRUITMENT

Social media has three main purposes for recruitment: branding, digital advertising, and sourcing of candidates. Let's go into more detail about these three functions.

SOCIAL MEDIA AND THE TIE BETWEEN RECRUITMENT BRANDING

One great function of social media is its ability to grow your organization's recruitment brand. Social media's audience is engaged, active, and in real time, which can help grow your organization's recruitment brand.

It is important to have organizational pages on your social media sites dedicated to promoting your brand. You need original content that will attract and keep users of your brand. In many large organizations, this is a full-time role.

Posting jobs is part of the branding process but it should be secondary to content. Consumers will feel like they are being spammed if all you post are jobs.

Ideas for content to share include:

1. New Innovations
2. Interesting news
3. Awards
4. Organizational good deeds
5. Fun facts

SOCIAL MEDIA AS A DIGITAL ADVERTISING TOOL

A great use of social media is paid digital advertising. This is where an organization pays a fee to advertise jobs on another social media site. This works the same way on most social media sites. Basically, your sponsored content, such as a job posting, is promoted to users who you have set a criteria to find. Criteria can include location, job titles mentioned in their profiles, and interests which are similar to a job title.

SOCIAL MEDIA AS A SOURCING TOOL

Social media is also a place to research candidates and to connect with talent about job opportunities.

THE BIGGEST SOCIAL MEDIA SITES

Outlined below are some of the major social media sites; how to source on these sites; and how to leverage them for your organization's recruitment, branding, and digital advertising.

FACEBOOK
HTTPS://WWW.FACEBOOK.COM/

Facebook is the largest social media site, with over 1.65 billion active users and growing. It is also a great site for recruitment branding, digital ads and sourcing.

FACEBOOK RECRUITMENT BRANDING

Facebook is the most well-known of all social media sites and can have the biggest impact on your organization's recruitment brand due to the sheer number of users who interact with Facebook on a daily basis. For recruitment branding, it is essential that your organization have a professional-looking Facebook page. From this page, you grow your audience, which is similar to a talent community. To continue to build your audience, consistent content needs to be posted on a regular basis.

FACEBOOK DIGITAL ADS

Facebook has strict criteria and can be quite tedious, so it is recommended that you either leave it to an expert or learn to follow their criteria correctly. Basically, from your organization's Facebook page, you create content, such as an ad for a job. From there, you set the criteria for your audience (such as location and interest, which can be similar to a job title), set your budget and length of time you want the ad to run, and then launch the ad. Facebook has good analytics that allows you to see how your ad performs in terms of click rate.

FACEBOOK SOURCING

A big mistake many recruiters make is to post their jobs on their own personal Facebook wall, hoping their target audience reads the post. This will not attract many people other than maybe your Aunt Margaret. It's not the best way to reach your target audience. A more useful way to source candidates on Facebook is to use it as a research tool.

The first way to source talent is to join local domain-specific user groups in the area you are recruiting for. After you join, you can view a list of users, including many of the people you are hoping to recruit. Most of the larger professional organizations in the area you recruit for will most likely have a group on Facebook to join. Another way to find groups that possess the skills and experience you want to recruit for is to go to your Facebook group page section and look under "discovery." Or simply type in the area you are looking to recruit for and most likely some groups will pop up.

The second way to source talent on Facebook is to use it like LinkedIn, with a little slight variance. In the Facebook search bar, type in "People who like" and then what you are recruiting for and the location. An example would be "People who like nurses Florida." What will pop up will be a combination of nurse groups, as well as nurses and unrelated news. Any nurse groups and nurse profiles that pop up will provide leads. Another example would be to search for graduates of a particular school, like "people who graduate from Harvard in 2015." Most of the profiles that pop up will be people who graduated from Harvard in 2015.

Keep in mind that sourcing on Facebook has limitations and can be time consuming, so it should not be your go-to site.

LINKEDIN
HTTPS://WWW.LINKEDIN.COM/

LinkedIn is the world's largest professional social media site with over 433 million active users. LinkedIn grew at such a rapid pace that it was purchased by Microsoft in June 2016.

LINKEDIN RECRUITMENT BRANDING

LinkedIn allows organizations to build and create their own branded pages, called Career Pages. Like Facebook, this is a great way to grow your organization's brand. Please note that there is a cost on LinkedIn if you want to add your Career Page with listed jobs to your company page.

LINKEDIN DIGITAL ADS

LinkedIn has the ability to run targeted ads. The advantage to this is virtually all LinkedIn users can be identified by a job title and company, which means targeted digital ads can be effective.

LINKEDIN SOURCING

What separates LinkedIn from other social media is the advanced ability to both research and source. No other social media can compare to LinkedIn in this regard. One important point many recruiters forget about LinkedIn is: most LinkedIn profiles are not complete resumes, so most profiles will be missing pieces of information and skills. This means that many profiles will not pop up on searches because the user did not list that particular skill set.

PAID LINKEDIN SOURCING

The easiest and most effective way to source on LinkedIn is to pay for a LinkedIn Recruiter account. These accounts cost money, so recruiters have to ensure they use them effectively.

The two advantages of having a LinkedIn Recruiter account is to access virtually all users' information on LinkedIn, and to be able to send direct InMails to these users. Even with the most expensive Recruiter account, you are limited on how many users you can contact. Also you are rewarded by how many of these users accept your InMails, as they give you a credit back for every accepted InMail.

Although through a Recruiter account you can send an InMail to almost all users, just remember that many of the users are very passive so there is never a guarantee they will be interested in your roles. Also, in my own experience, some professions like sales and HR have a higher response rate compared to areas like health care.

HOW TO SEARCH FOR CANDIDATES WITH A PAID RECRUITER ACCOUNT

The paid Recruiter account allows for advanced search functions and is quite easy to learn and use. You can set up your search criteria by job title, company, keywords, and location, to name a few. After you find the profiles you like, you can send InMails about opportunities and if they respond, you can connect with them outside of the system. The InMails only allow for limited words, sort of like the old want ads, so you have to choose your words carefully.

HOW TO SEARCH FOR FREE ON LINKEDIN

When searching for free on LinkedIn, you will have to become more creative in how you search, as you will not have complete access to all profile and search options.

The first option is to merely use the search that is provided for free on LinkedIn. The search options and the amount of profiles you can view will be limited, and you will not see past your third connections.

The second option is a LinkedIn X-ray search. Basically, using search commands on Google, you can find LinkedIn profiles. You will learn more about advanced Boolean commands in the sourcing chapter.

An example of how to find a basic profile based on skills and location would be:

site:ca.linkedin.com "java developer" and Toronto -jobs

A more advanced search based on location and skill set targeting directories would be:

site:www.linkedin.com intitle:linkedin J2EE and Ohio -intitle:answers -intitle:updated -intitle:blog -intitle:directory -inurl:jobs

The third option is to use a free tool called https://recruitin. net/. This great tool allows you to search on LinkedIn by doing an X-ray search for you to save time. It also allows you to search by country, location, keywords and education.

CONNECTING WITH CANDIDATES YOU FIND ON LINKEDIN WITHOUT A PAID RECRUITER ACCOUNT

In almost all cases on LinkedIn, you have access to your first connections' email contact information.

When you see a profile you like, if they are not a first connection, you will have to figure out their work email and/or work phone number combinations in order reach out to them. In the sourcing section, you will learn more about how to find emails and phone combinations.

GET YOUR HIRING MANAGERS TO RECRUIT ON LINKEDIN

Many recruiters waste hours posting their jobs on their own LinkedIn page. If you were to ask these recruiters, very few actually get hires for hard-to-fill roles from this method. A better way to post jobs on LinkedIn is to have your hiring managers post their jobs. Hiring managers are most likely connected to a LinkedIn network of professionals like themselves, who will more readily respond to someone they know as opposed to a recruiter they do not.

LINKEDIN JOB POSTINGS

LinkedIn also allows for traditional paid job postings. It is a way to post jobs to LinkedIn's huge social media audience.

TWITTER
HTTPS://TWITTER.COM/

Twitter is a social media site where users can send out short messages. The site is very popular among celebrities and has over 300 million active users.

TWITTER RECRUITMENT BRANDING

With many loyal followers, Twitter is a great place to grow an organization's career brand. You can create a business profile and send out messages about your career brand, all free.

TWITTER DIGITAL ADS

Similar to LinkedIn and Facebook, Twitter allows you to create paid digital ads. Through your business account, you can create a job ad and target audiences that are in the same location and have similar interests to the job you are posting.

TWITTER SOURCING

Twitter, like most social media, should not be your go-to sourcing site—nonetheless, it can be a source for finding candidates.

There are different ways to research candidates on Twitter, such as finding them on their group or association pages, using Boolean search strings, and using free Twitter search sites. Below are examples for each:

FIND CANDIDATES ON THEIR GROUP AND ASSOCIATION TWITTER PAGES

The easiest way to locate candidates on Twitter is to find group and association Twitter pages. One way to find groups on Twitter is to type in the professional you are looking for in the Twitter search bar (https://twitter.com/search-advanced?lang=en). An example would be "registered nurse" and other nurse-related words in the advanced search section. An additional tip for finding groups and associations on Twitter is to go to the home pages on large association websites and find their Twitter link.

USE BOOLEAN TO FIND CANDIDATES ON TWITTER

Having several effective Boolean Twitter searches can make the difference between finding a few profiles and finding a generous number of potential candidates to contact. Below are some Boolean Twitter search examples:

Example 1 - Use tweets and replies to find nurses, such as -- site: twitter.com "tweets and replies" registered nurse

Example 2 - The above example you can also type in as -- specialty site: twitter.com "tweets and replies" Registered nurse "Icu"

Example 3 - Simple Old-School X-Ray Search -- site: twitter. com (rn OR "registered nurse") (dallas OR texas).

Example 4 - Use https://recruitin.net/twitter.php and it will do all the work for you.

YOUTUBE
HTTPS://WWW.YOUTUBE.COM/

YouTube is a social media site where users can post videos and people can make comments. YouTube has over one billion viewers each month so it has an enormous audience.

YOUTUBE RECRUITMENT BRANDING

Videos are a great way to promote a brand, and no social media site does a better job of posting and promoting videos than YouTube. Organizations can create their own free pages to promote their recruitment branded videos. This can attract followers to their brand. Videos hosted on YouTube can be used in other recruitment marketing efforts, such as career pages. Also, emails can be sent to candidates about jobs.

YOUTUBE DIGITAL ADS

The neat thing about YouTube digital ads is that they are mostly video-related, which grabs viewers' attention. You can create an ad based on subject matter and viewers' locations. For example, you can set an ad to run in Phoenix, Arizona on a CPA training course with lots of views. This could attract a CPA watching the course who sees your ad.

YOUTUBE SOURCING

YouTube also is the weakest of the social media sites for sourcing and research, but some hidden gems can be found on YouTube. One way to find candidates is to type the domain you are looking for in the YouTube search bar. Different videos related to your subject will pop up. From there, look in the comment section and you will find some individuals who have made comments related to the domain you are looking for. If you look closer, some of these commenters are professionals in the industry you are searching and potential candidates to connect with.

WHY GLASSDOOR MATTERS

When looking for a product or service, the majority of consumers today read reviews before making a purchasing decision. Job seekers are no different and the number one place they look for reviews on a potential employer is Glassdoor.

WHAT IS GLASSDOOR?

Glassdoor - https://www.glassdoor.com/index.htm - is the top employee review website where current or past employees give reviews about their experiences working at an organization. The employees giving the review can score up to five stars, with five being high and one being low. Along with the reviews, employees can make comments.

WHY CARE ABOUT YOUR ORGANIZATION'S GLASSDOOR RATING?

More and more job seekers will look up a potential employer's score and comments on Glassdoor. If an employer has a low score and bad comments, there is a good chance that a potential candidate will not be interested in the job offered to them by the recruiter. Basically, recruiters who work for organizations that continue to ignore their low Glassdoor ratings will be less successful in recruiting talent.

HOW TO IMPROVE YOUR ORGANIZATION GLASSDOOR RATING?

The best way to improve your Glassdoor scores and comments is to encourage your organization to ask employees with positive experiences to give positive reviews and write good comments on Glassdoor. Do not be afraid that employees will not want to take the time to give a good rating. Many employees with positive opinions of an organization are proud and loyal to their organization and will not have a problem taking the time to give a good rating and make positive comments. You will also be surprised how easy and fast it is to improve a low Glassdoor rating just by directly asking employees.

HOW TO USE A POSITIVE GLASSDOOR RATING ON GLASSDOOR TO ATTRACT CANDIDATES

Glassdoor is also one of the fastest-growing websites where candidates search for jobs. If you have a good Glassdoor score, it is a good site to post jobs. Glassdoor does charge to have your jobs posted, so you want to make sure your scores are high on the site.

RECRUITMENT MARKETING - TIPS ON PAID JOB BOARDS

Paid job postings on job boards have been around for close to twenty years and should still have a big place in your recruitment marketing plan. Following are some tips on job postings, as well as how to be effective when posting your jobs on some of the more well-known sites.

DO NOT PUT ALL OF YOUR EGGS IN ONE BASKET

When it comes to paid job postings, it is important that you do not put all your eggs into one basket and just use one site. Think of people who drink only one soft drink. Job boards can be similar in that if you focus only on one site, you could miss candidates who use other job boards.

MOST NICHE SITES ARE WORTHLESS

There are many niche job sites in almost every major industry. The majority of these sites will not pull a great return on investment and should be avoided.

BUY A SMALL SAMPLE SIZE AND EXPAND FROM THERE

When it comes to paid job postings, it is recommended you do a small sample size first and if you get good results, you can expand from there.

MONITOR PERFORMANCES

It is absolutely paramount that you monitor the performances of your paid job postings to see if this is a good investment worth continuing.

WHAT DOES A GOOD RETURN ON INVESTMENT LOOK LIKE?

ROI on a great paid job posting would be under $1,000 per hire. If it is an average performing paid job posting, the ROI is under $2,000 per hire. Anything over $3,000 per paid job posting is a poor performing tool that you should stop using.

ASK VENDORS FOR TIPS AND HELP

Most vendors want to help you be successful because you will likely invest more in their job posting products. Therefore, many will give you valuable tips and training on how to improve using their job posting products.

SOME OF THE MAJOR JOB BOARDS WITH JOB POSTING TIPS

CAREERBUILDER
HTTP://WWW.CAREERBUILDER.COM/

CareerBuilder, one of the longest running job boards, has a loyal following among some job seekers, and it can be advantageous to reach this audience.

TIPS FOR POSTING ON CAREERBUILDER

1. CareerBuilder is very SEO centric; therefore, follow the lessons you learned in SEO training.
2. CareerBuilder allows for short applications and this is recommended.
3. Do not post CareerBuilder through your applicant tracking system. In many cases ATSs will be too long of an application process.
4. Use branded postings to get more engagement. Branded postings, available in the professional or premium posting packages, are a paid option from CareerBuilder in which they allow the use of your organization's branded logo with a job posting. Skin effects are more visually appealing compared to text-looking job postings. These packages come with a company profile page that allows employers to elaborate on their organization, what it's like to work there, and list any unique benefits they offer employees.
5. The best time to post on CareerBuilder is mid-week.

INDEED
HTTP://WWW.INDEED.COM/

Indeed is the largest job site with over 180 million unique visitors each month and growing. Indeed is different than any other job board—it works more like a search engine than a traditional job board.

1. Research and look at your competitors. Look to see who typically ranks first among your competitors and try to copy their posting format to achieve the same success.
2. Try to follow and understand Indeed's algorithms when posting sponsored jobs. For the best results, avoid numbers and symbols in job titles.
3. Do not sponsor Indeed jobs through your ATS. Applicant tracking systems tend to have long application processes which most job seekers disdain.
4. Do not post in cities too close to each other. As sponsored jobs on Indeed are pay-per-click, having two jobs in the same market will compete against each other.
5. Use short application job postings. You will increase the number of candidates you receive; job seekers like an easy and fast application process.

MONSTER
HTTP://WWW.MONSTER.COM/

Monster is one of the original career sites, and has built up a loyal following over the years.

1. Do not post Monster jobs through your ATS. Applicant tracking systems tend to have long application processes, which most job seekers

disdain. Applying directly on Monster simplifies the application process, getting you more candidates.

2. Use Monster-centric job titles. Monster has a preference for specific titles that they have researched over the years. Look at what titles are being used for your roles and use those.

3. Monster's best time for posting, like CareerBuilder, is mid-week as opposed to the end or beginning of the week.

4. Use short application job postings. You will increase the amount of candidates you receive—job seekers like easy and fast processes.

ZIPRECRUITER
HTTPS://WWW.ZIPRECRUITER.COM/

ZipRecruiter is one of the fastest-growing job boards. It works differently from most job boards, posting your jobs to over a hundred job boards/websites.

TIPS FOR POSTING ON ZIPRECRUITER

1. ZipRecruiter gives you an option to include your company logo, which gets you more hits.
2. Post a map of your location. Job postings with maps on ZipRecruiter get more views.
3. Follow traditional SEO when posting on ZipRecruiter.
4. Repost your job every 30 days to keep it fresh.
5. Post directly via ZipRecruiter, not through your ATS.

FREE JOB POSTINGS & AGGREGATORS

The best things in life are free. That old saying applies to marketing your jobs. There are some great ways you can market your jobs without spending a single penny.

JOB AGGREGATORS PROVIDE THE BEST FREE MARKETING

Possibly the greatest thing ever created for recruiters was the job aggregator, which promotes all of your jobs for free.

Job aggregators are essentially job board search engines that collect job postings across the internet and make them easily searchable. For most job aggregators, there are usually paid and free options available.

WELL-KNOWN JOB AGGREGATORS

1. **Indeed** - http://www.indeed.com/ This is by far the largest job aggregator in the world. Most of the world's job postings get indexed through Indeed. Indeed offers two free options, one for large or mid-sized organizations and one for small organizations. For large organizations, Indeed collects all jobs you have posted in your applicant tracking systems. For small organizations, you have the option to post directly on Indeed.

2. **Juju** - https://www.juju.com This is a smaller version of Indeed and also offers a free option to post jobs.

FREE JOB POSTING SITES

There are many places you can post your jobs for free. It is recommended that you experiment with these sites to see what works in your industry. Below is a list of free job posting sites with links and brief descriptions.

1. **Craigslist** - https://www.craigslist.org/about/sites An online classifieds section, posting jobs is still free in smaller locations.
2. **Job Spider** - http://www.jobspider.com/ Similar to Craigslist, this site allows free job posting.
3. **Post Jobs For Free** - http://www.postjobfree.com/ A small free job aggregator.
4. **Trovit** - https://www.trovit.com/ A free classified job posting site.
5. **US.jobs** - http://us.jobs/indexingrequest.asp This is a federal government site where you can post jobs for free.
6. **State Sponsored Job Boards** – Many states have government-sponsored sites which allow employers to post for free. An example in Florida: ishttps://www.employflorida.com/vosnet/Default.aspx
7. **College and Alumni Job boards** – Most schools allow you to post to grads and alumni.
8. **Backpage** - http://www.backpage.com/ This is a free job classified site.
9. **Stackjobs** - https://stackjobs.co.uk/ A free UK-focused job posting site.
10. **Hire Up** - http://www.gogohireup.com/post-jobs-for-free A free job site specializing in technology.
11. **Veterans Employment Center** - https://www.vets.

gov/employment/employers/ The site allows you to post jobs for Veterans.

12. **Needjobsoon** - http://www.needjobsoon.com/ employer A free job posting site.

13. Oodle - http://www.oodle.com/ A free classified job posting site.

6:
YOUR OWN PERSONAL RECRUITMENT BRAND

An area that rarely gets covered, yet one that is important for recruiters, is developing a personal brand. In this chapter, I will discuss why building your own personal brand is important and how to create and grow your own personal recruitment brand.

WHAT IS A PERSONAL RECRUITMENT BRAND?

Personal recruitment brand is the way recruiters create awareness and information about themselves as a recruiter. This is also completely separate from their corporate recruitment branding.

WHY IS BUILDING YOUR PERSONAL

RECRUITMENT BRAND IMPORTANT?

When a candidate looks into an organization, not only do they go to Glassdoor to find out about the company, they also look at recruiters' LinkedIn profiles and other related information. If a recruiter has no personal brand, candidates trust them less and will be less likely to respond to their job inquiries.

Another benefit of building your own personal brand is that if you grow your brand to a high level, candidates will find you, which makes recruiting much easier.

A final benefit of building your own personal brand is the chance to build equity in your long-term marketability as a recruiter. The more people know about you in the industry, the more likely you will grow your career in the recruitment business.

LINKEDIN: THE MOST IMPORTANT PLACE FOR YOUR RECRUITMENT BRANDING

One of the most important aspects of a recruiter's personal branding is their LinkedIn profile. Many candidates, when contacted by a recruiter, will look at that recruiter's profile to determine if the recruiter is a real person working for a real company. The more background information that a recruiter has on LinkedIn, the more a candidate will feel the recruiter is a real person. Having a picture on LinkedIn is a must as it shows what you look like, which will add to your credibility.

HOW TO GROW YOUR OWN PERSONAL RECRUITMENT BRAND ON LINKEDIN

In order to grow your brand on LinkedIn, it is recommended that you connect with LinkedIn users. Below are some ways to increase the number of people to connect with:

1. Look up people you know on LinkedIn and ask them to join your network. This includes current and past colleagues.
2. Send out invites to people you know who you think can benefit from LinkedIn. LinkedIn can even send out email invites for you through your Hotmail, Gmail or Outlook contacts.
3. Connect with recruiters. Most recruiters will accept your request; strengthening your connection with other recruiters is a great way to grow your influence in the industry.
4. Connect with candidates in your field. Be careful on this one—LinkedIn will warn you if you try to connect to too many people who reject your request to add them to your network.

SEARCH OPTIMIZE YOUR LINKEDIN PROFILE SO THE CANDIDATE WILL FIND YOU

Similar to search optimizing a job description, adding

keywords to your profile can help candidates find you. This also shows you have expertise in the area you are recruiting for. Here are some quick tips:

1. Recruiter should be your title, as that's how most candidates search for recruiters.
2. You should put your specialty in your job title. Example: Technical Recruiter or Nurse Recruiter.
3. Put keywords in your job description about your specialty area.
4. Write your company name as people would search for it. If people do not know it by its abbreviation, then write out it out in full or how most candidates will recognize it.

OTHER WAYS TO GROW YOUR PERSONAL RECRUITMENT BRAND

1. **Your business email personal signature.** This is going to sound elementary, but recruiters have to have proper information in their email signatures as part of their personal brand. When you reach out to candidates, if they have to figure out who you are they may not want to work with you. To ensure you are branded properly in your email, your email signature should include your full name, title, company and your social media links.
2. **Have profiles on other social media sites – Twitter, Google+, & Facebook.** Having presence on other

social media sites can help expand your personal recruitment brand.

3. **Post relevant content not just job postings.** Send out relevant content, such as industry news, instead of just job postings. This will keep your social media connections more engaged with your brand.

CONCLUSION

Do not make the same mistake that many recruiters do by not creating your own personal recruitment brand. By creating a personal recruitment brand, you will create awareness and increase your presence as a recruiter. This, in turn, will allow candidates to be aware of who you are and what you do as a recruiter.

7:
SOURCING

- RETURN ON TIME
- RESEARCH
- BOOLEAN 101, ATS/CRM – YOUR HIDDEN GOLD MINE
- HOW TO GET THE MOST OUT OF PAID RESUME DATABASE
- OPEN WEB SOURCING
- ADVANCED NETWORKING
- HOW TO FIND COMPANY EMAILS & PHONE NUMBERS

Sourcing is the art of finding and attracting candidates through a multitude of innovative techniques. Sourcing serves a vital role in recruitment due to the fact that for many hard-to-fill roles there are very few applicants. With candidates not directly applying for these jobs, it is paramount that recruiters learn how to research, solicit and engage these candidates. This chapter will provide a broad background in many sourcing techniques that will help you to fill those hard-to-fill roles.

*Please note: screen shots will not be used in this chapter, as some of the sites listed did not give sign-off approval. Therefore, for standardization purposes, screen shots will not be used for examples of searches in this chapter.

RETURN ON TIME (ROT)

Sourcing can be a very time-consuming endeavor, and the difference between an average recruiter and an advanced expert is often the speed at which they search. In order to improve your speed, you have to perfect your Return on Time (ROT) sourcing.

ROT, from a sourcing perspective, is the art of how to improve your sourcing speed through a set of steps that ensures your time is focused on techniques and tools that maximize your sourcing time.

ROT sourcing is my main innovation and contribution to sourcing. I have helped hundreds of recruiters improve in this area through my articles, training programs and seminars. By learning the concepts of ROT, a recruiter will develop the skill set needed to be successful in sourcing.

Please read this section carefully—this this could be the fundamental game-changer in your career. Improving your sourcing speed through ROT training will make you a superior practitioner of the sourcing arts. Below you will learn how to increase the speed of your sourcing to become an advanced expert.

WHY IS RETURN ON TIME (ROT) IMPORTANT?

The second a sourcer goes live working on a req, there is a high probability that other external sourcers are working on the very same req and going after the same candidates. Whoever creates the most accurate strategy and has the fastest speed to reach out to the small pool of candidates will be the most successful. With speed being such an important part of sourcing, learning to master your sourcing speed can truly make you a great sourcer.

THE FIRST STEP FOR ROT IS TO KNOW YOUR HOURS TO SUBMISSION RATIO

The first step to understand ROT is to figure out how many hours it takes you to get a submission. This changes from industry to industry, but the industry average time to get a submission for hard-to-fill roles is eight hours, according to leading recruitment analytical expert David Szary of Lean Human Capital.

To figure out your hours to submission ratio, first calculate how many submissions you get in a month in the core sourcing hours worked. For example, if you worked 160 hours but only 100 of those hours were spent sourcing, then you would have 100 core sourcing hours. Then take those core sourcing hours worked (100) and divide it by the submissions you had that month.

The final equation would look like this: 100 core sourcing hours worked divided by 25 monthly submissions equals 4 hours worked per submission. Once you know how many hours it takes to get a submission, you can look at techniques to improve that number by decreasing your sourcing time.

10 WAYS TO INCREASE YOUR SOURCING SPEED & IMPROVE YOUR RETURN ON TIME METRIC

1. The order in which you search

By increasing the speed with which you source, you will have the potential to double your recruitment production levels. The best way to increase your sourcing speed is to prioritize the order in which you search. By merely changing the order in which you search, you can effectively save days in finding qualified candidates. It is recommended to first use tools and techniques that give you the biggest return on your time. The basic rule of thumb is the warmer the lead, the more likely a candidate will be interested in your role. Following is the recommended order:

1) Pre-existing candidates
2) People who apply to your posts
3) Recent applicants in your Applicant Tracking System/CRM
4) Recent applicants to job boards
5) Past applicants in your Applicant Tracking System/CRM
6) Old applicants on job boards
7) LinkedIn In-Mail
8) Networking
9) Boolean searches on the internet
10) Cold calling competitors.

2. Learn to Read Resumes and Information Faster

Many people have heard of the term speed reading. Applying some speed reading techniques to reading resumes and processing information can be a quick way to improve your ROT score.

Tips for speed reading include the following:

- Learn to work faster. If you have a natural tendency to move slowly, you have to learn that to be successful at sourcing, you have to move fast. In sourcing, taking your time will only result in your competitor contacting candidates before you do!

- Doing resume and information reading search drills. Every day for two weeks, keep track of the time you spent going through resumes on a job board or an online Boolean search. Each day try to do it faster than the day before. Over time this score will lower.
- Focus on scanning key words; don't read every word. When looking for information, reading every word can be a huge time consumer. It is better to focus on scanning information.
- Get better at understanding what information you are looking for. Once you are a domain expert, you will understand what you are looking for, which helps you process information faster.
- Lower distractions. To move fast, you must concentrate on information that is important. Therefore, avoid excessive chatter and other stimuli. A good recommendation is to listen to music.

3.   Cut Out Boolean Strings that Do Not Produce.

Boolean, done correctly, can lead a recruiter/sourcer to a gold mine of candidates. On the flip side, Boolean strings done ineffectively wastes valuable time. Constantly monitor the time you spend on a search – on a micro level. If a particular search string is not effectively producing candidates, move on to other Boolean strings and tools.

4.   Indeed

Indeed is one of the best tools for speed, as its resume database was designed for speed. On Indeed's database, recruiters can quickly read a candidate's entire profile on one page. At the same time, recruiters can quickly click profiles they like and instantaneously send up to 50 in-mails to potential candidates. If a recruiter focuses on Indeed, he or she can easily send out a thousand in-mails to candidates in one day. It would be hard to find similar tools which allow a recruiter to connect with the volume of candidates that quickly. In addition, Indeed has one of the largest resume databases, which makes it a great place to search for candidates.

5. Do Not Spend Excessive Hours Experimenting on New Tools

One of the fun aspects of sourcing is the ability to experiment with new tools and techniques. In order to advance in knowledge, there has to be a place for experimentation. Too much experimentation, however, can result in the loss of valuable sourcing hours. Experimenting should be kept on the sidelines instead of being the focus of your time.

6. Text candidates

To contact candidates faster, text them. Some people do not instantly respond to phone or email but look at texts right away. By texting, you might get a hold of candidates faster, thus speeding up your ability to source. When texting a mass volume of candidates, look to texting through CRM and Software Texting programs. Not having to text candidates one at a time saves hours of labor.

7. Get better at recycling candidates

An easy way to increase your sourcing speed is by getting better at recycling candidates. A recruiter can save hundreds of sourcing hours just by knowing who is in their recent pipeline.

Many times, a recruiter has candidates who are not a fit for one job but are great for another. Remembering and keeping track of these candidates can take only a few minutes and result in a submission.

8.   Do Accurate Intakes

Doing accurate intakes will enable you to understand the exact needs of your hiring managers and will prevent you from focusing time on inappropriate candidate profiles. Doing inaccurate intakes wastes time and has a massive negative impact on your ROT.

9.   Use Better Engagement Techniques

Having better engagement of how many candidates respond to your solicitations can speed up your sourcing. The industry standard for candidates' replies to solicitations is around 25% for local candidates. If your score is less than that, a lot of your labor-intensive sourcing might be not effective. Improving how candidates respond to your engagement will result in getting more bang for your sourcing time. If your current response rate is only 10% and you double it, then you can accomplish the same amount of work in half the time.

10.   Use CRMs or Email Campaign Software

You can save hours of time by doing mass email campaigns through CRMs or email campaign software. These tools save so much time because they allow the sourcer or recruiter to target an exponential amount of candidates, as compared to singular manual emails.

ROT CONCLUSION

By applying these tips on how to increase your sourcing speed, you will decrease the time it takes to submit a candidate, which will improve your ROT metric. This, in turn, can be the difference between being an average recruiter and an advanced practitioner.

RESEARCH

The research component of sourcing is the ability to use various sources to find candidates. Below are some of the common tools recruiters use to find candidates.

1. **ATS/CRM Systems** – These are the systems that house candidates who have either previously applied for jobs or who have previously been researched.
2. **Job Boards** – These are mostly paid sites where a recruiter can search for candidates who have submitted their resumes to be searched by the public. Examples of major job boards include CareerBuilder, Indeed, Monster, and Ziprecruiter, plus hundreds of smaller and niche-based boards.
3. **LinkedIn** – The largest business social media site where a huge percentage of the working population has a profile. Great place to research candidates.
4. **Social media** – With most of the world's population on social media, many candidates have profiles, which makes this a great place to research candidates.

5. **Free industry association online directories** – There are many free industry-specific online directories. Most of these directories are not intended for recruiters but for the public looking to find a professional. These directories are usually profession-specific. In some cases, you can search for virtually everyone who holds a license within that profession.

6. **Hard copy directory books** - These mostly paid services were the forerunner to the internet. These physical directory books list key people in specific professions.

7. **Paid online directories** – These sites can provide information on professionals you are looking for. Examples of these sites include ZoomInfo, Data.com, and Hoovers.

8. **Talent mapping** – This is where you call into an organization to map out the key people you are looking to recruit. Some recruiters pay third parties to get them names. This is called name generation.

9. **Conference attendee lists** - Many professionals attend conferences, which list the attendees' names. Some of these lists are free online or you can pay a small free to obtain either the online or physical copies.

10. **Open web Boolean searches** - For this technique, you use various search commands on the web to find people.

BOOLEAN 101

If you are not familiar with Boolean, it involves using sequences of word commands in databases or search engines to find information. Boolean is a fundamental tool of sourcing and can help you find information faster and more accurately.

BASIC BOOLEAN COMMANDS

The first step in mastering Boolean is to understand basic Boolean commands. There are eight main basic Boolean operators: AND, OR, NOT, Near, ( ), "", site, and inurl

1. **AND** - This command links two things together when doing a search. For example: C++ AND capital markets. This would prompt a search of C++ and capital markets together. This is good way for adding things to a search.
2. **OR** – This command can link words together when doing a search. For example: RN OR Registered Nurse. This would prompt a search for either RN or Registered Nurse. This is a good time-saver as some things are searched two ways.
3. **NOT** – This command means you want to exclude a specific word when doing a search. For example, you want to have the word engineer but want to exclude the word engineering. For this search, you would type: Engineer NOT engineering. This is a good way to exclude things from a search.
4. **Near** – This command means you want words to

appear near each other. For example ICU and nurse. If ICU and nurse are found close together, this command will find them. This search would look like this: ICU Near Nurse. This search is great at finding things that go together that might not have be written together.

5. **() Brackets** – This command will focus on whatever word is placed in your bracket. For example if you write J2EE in a bracket such as: (J2EE) the focus of the search will be on J2EE.

6. **"" Quotations** – This command finds exact phrases together. For example, if you want to find a Pharmaceutical Sales Representative focusing only on these words together, you would type: "Pharmaceutical Sales Representative".

7. **site:** - Limits your search to one domain such as site:LinkedIn.

8. **inurl:** - Limits your search to words found in a URL, such as the word resume.

ATS/CRM – YOUR HIDDEN GOLD MINE

WHAT ARE ATS AND CRMS?

ATS - stands for applicant tracking system. ATSs are systems designed to store, track, audit, and move candidates through the whole recruiting life cycle.

CRM – stands for customer relationship management.

CRMs are systems designed to store and track candidates. These systems are usually better at searching and making contact with candidates than ATSs.

WHY SOURCE IN YOUR ATS/CRM?

Almost every recruitment department has some form of a ATS/CRM system. In most of these systems are dormant candidates who have shown previous interest in your brand.

Many times, candidates who apply are disqualified by both system and human error. Other times, silver medalist candidates who interviewed well are dispositioned after another candidate is chosen during the interview process.

Many of these candidates are perfect fits for roles but by inadvertent errors are lost in your ATS/CRM.

TIPS FOR SEARCHING IN ATSs

Most ATSs have poor Boolean search capabilities, as they are designed more for moving candidates through the recruitment life cycle as opposed to searching for candidates. That being the case, there are some ways to search for candidates in your ATS without Boolean. Below is a quick list of tips for searching in your ATS:

1. Look up jobs similar to the one you are working on. In these jobs, look at candidates who made it to final stages and were not hired by your organization.
2. Look at candidate folders. If your organization uses candidate folders, you can search the folder to see if

there are any viable candidates.

3. Try to match candidates outside the ATS and match them to the ATS. If candidates have applied to ATS jobs, they are more likely to be warmer leads as they will be familiar with your brand.

4. Look up old reqs for junior roles. The individuals not selected a few years back for your junior roles most likely are doing the similar role at an intermediate level at your competitors. Some of these candidates might have grown into viable candidates, so it is worth a shot to connect with them.

TIPS FOR SEARCHING IN CRMs

Properly built CRMs are designed to find candidates easily. Many ATSs have millions of profiles that are hard to find. This is why many organizations use CRMs with or withstanding of an applicant tracking system. Below you will find a quick list of tips for searching in your CRMS:

1. Use Boolean search commands to find the profile you are looking for.

2. Search under lists. Many CRMs have candidates filed under lists.

3. Search under tags. Many CRMs have candidates filed under tags.

4. Search under folders. Many CRMs have candidates filed under folders.

5. Search under old jobs. In these jobs, look at candidates who made it to the final stages of an interview and were not hired by your organization.

6. Look up old junior profiles. These individuals most likely are now at an intermediate level working for your competitors. Some of these candidates might have grown into viable candidates so it is worth a shot to connect with them.

HOW TO RE-ENGAGE WITH YOUR ATS/CRM CANDIDATES

Re-engaging with ATS/CRM candidates could make for easy hires if they are engaged the right way. Contact the candidate using all available contact information you have on them. In your first re-engagement, the first thing that should be brought up is their past interest in your organization.

EXTRA CRM TIPS

1. **Mass contact candidates in your CRM.** The great thing about most CRMs is they allow you to send out mass emails at one time. From a speed-sourcing perspective, this tool can save hours by allowing you to contact thousands of contacts in a short period of time.

2. **Hoard all candidate information in your CRM.** Any information about candidates should be stored in your CRM. By doing this over time, you will add valuable extra candidates that you can search for later.

ATS/CRM CONCLUSION

By actively targeting qualified candidates who have previously applied to your organization, you will see an uptick in hires that will cost zero marketing dollars.

HOW TO GET THE MOST OUT OF PAID RESUME DATABASES

Paid resume databases should be utilized in most organizations' sourcing plans. Although paid resume databases are important, if not used correctly they can be a big expense with no return on your investment. This section will look at some of the bigger resume databases and how to best use them.

CAREERBUILDER RESUME DATABASE

CareerBuilder is one of the longest-running job boards, and has a loyal following among job seekers. Below are some great tips on how to find candidates using the CareerBuilder resume database.

BASIC CAREERBUILDER SEARCH

From CareerBuilder's Employer Desktop, you are given three fields to use to search the resume database: keyword, location and last activity. If you wanted to search for a financial advisor in New York who recently applied, you would type "financial advisor" or "financial planner" under keyword. For location, you would type in "New York". For last activity, you would type "last month."

MORE ADVANCED CAREERBUILDER TIPS

CareerBuilder allows you to do an advanced search with or without Boolean. CareerBuilder also has many filters. Some filters may not be applicable for all searches but can be utilized for more specific types of searches. Here are some tips for each of the main filters:

1. **Keywords** – This section is great for either basic keywords or Boolean queries. For example: (ICU or "intensive care") and (PCU or "progressive care").
2. **Location** (miles drop down) - This section lets you select the location by city and ZIP/postal code.
3. **Country** (drop down) – Select the country you want to search in.
4. **Resume freshness** – Drop down with date (check either last activity or last modified), you select the time period to search, from one day to all resumes.
5. **Company name** – You can select one or more company name. Example: IBM or Oracle.
6. **Job title** – You can select one or more job titles. Example: "business analyst" or "system analyst".
7. **Categories** (drop down) – You can select different job categories.
8. **Salary, hourly or yearly** – (Check box to exclude

resumes that don't include salary) – Self-explanatory.

9. **Employment Type** (Check box full-time/part-time, contractor, intern, seasonal/temp) - Self-explanatory.

10. **Education** - You select a post-secondary school you want to search for.

11. **Minimum degree and maximum degree** (drop down) – You select the lowest level of education up to the highest level of education.

12. **Experience** – You select the amount of years of experience.

13. **Minimum level of travel** (drop down) - You select the amount of travel you would want the candidate to do.

14. **Should this candidate be currently employed?** (check box: yes, no, either) - Self-explanatory.

15. **Should this candidate have management experience?** (check box: yes, no, either) - Self-explanatory.

16. **What should be the minimum number of employees managed?** - Self-explanatory.

17. **Languages** (drop down of different languages) - Self-explanatory.

18. **Work status** (check box) - Self-explanatory.

19. **Security clearance** (check box) - Self-explanatory.

20. **Military experience** (check box) - Self-explanatory.

EXAMPLE OF AN ADVANCED CAREERBUILDER SEARCH

Below is an example of how to use CareerBuilder to find a ICU registered nurse or RN in Miami, who also has PCU experience

RECRUITING 101

with a degree, and has posted their resume in the past year:

1. **Keywords** – You would type (ICU or "intensive care") and (PCU or "Progressive care") – This will find both ICU and PCU experience as well as search for two versions of both experiences.
2. **Location** (miles drop down) – You would select the city of Miami with a dropdown of 20 miles.
3. **Country** (drop down) – United States
4. **Resume freshness** – You would select the drop down of last modified within the last year.
5. **Job title** – You would select RN or "registered nurse" – this will pull both of these common nursing titles.
6. **Minimum degree and maximum degree** - You would select the drop down as degree.

INDEED RESUME SEARCH

Indeed has grown in the past few years to be one of the biggest resume databases in the world. This growth has been triggered due to job seekers finding Indeed through its vast aggregated job network. Below you will find some great tips on how to search Indeed.

BASIC INDEED SEARCH

For the basic Indeed search, type in the keyword in the What section and select a location. So the basic search might be "Java" in the What section and "Chicago" in the Location section.

MORE ADVANCED INDEED SEARCHES

For the advanced Indeed search, you can select options to refine your search. Many of the Indeed searchable items work like Boolean, but Indeed does all the work for you. Below you will find some tips for each of the main searchable areas:

1. **All of these words** – All the words you type here will pop up in your search.
2. **The exact phrase** – Like Boolean quotations, it will put exact phrases into your search.
3. **At least one of these words** – This will ensure a specific word will appear in your search.
4. **None of these words** – Like the Boolean "not," it will remove a word from your search.
5. **Title of last job** – It allows you to search by the candidate's last job title.
6. **Title of any job** – It allows you to search by any job the candidate has had.
7. **Company of latest job** – It allows you to search by the candidate's latest company.
8. **Company of any job** – It allows you to search by the company the candidate has worked at.
9. **Years of work experience** (drop down) – Allows you to search by years of work experience.
10. **School name** – Allows you to search by a school the candidate has attended.
11. **Degree** (drop down) - Allows you to search by level of education.
12. **Field of study** - Allows you to search by a field of study.
13. **City, state, or ZIP** – Allows you to search by city,

state or ZIP code.

EXAMPLE OF AN ADVANCED INDEED SEARCH

Below is an example of how to use Indeed to find a store manager in Dallas who has a degree:

1. **Title of last job** –store manager
2. **Degree** (Drop down) - drop down to degree
3. **City, state, or ZIP** – Dallas

EXTRA INDEED SEARCH TIPS

1. Indeed is one of the few sites that you do not have to follow Boolean strings on.
2. Indeed searches the same way as how people think. That being the case, human logic is more important than Boolean. Think of different words and titles and search by those. Keep in mind that job tiles are called different things regionally, so search for both titles. A good example of this is nursing; in some areas "emergency department" is used while other regions use "emergency room."
3. Keep your search simple at first and then expand it. Start with just keywords, such as "J2EE". If that brings up too many candidates, then add filters and other keywords.
4. If your search doesn't produce results or if you can't find people who have not been contacted, change your search criteria.

MONSTER - POWER RESUME SEARCH & CLASSIC RESUME SEARCH

As part of its recruiting platform, Monster maintains one of the oldest and most well-known of all job boards and has a loyal following among some candidates. Monster also has two databases that can produce separate candidate searches: Power Resume Search & Classic Resume Search. Below you will find some great tips for searching in both databases:

POWER RESUME SEARCH

Monsters's Power Resume Search was built to try to make it easier for recruiters to search for resumes. The database has a built-in search that uses semantic capabilities – in other words, it searches against concepts that surface via common keywords. For example, a search for a concept like "human resources" will return resumes with hundreds of matching skills, including things like "recruiting/staffing/hiring," "compensation and benefits," and "workforce planning."

Basically, as you type a word, if it is common it will pop up as you search for that word. Also note that some of the search options will not be applicable to some searches but rather to specific types of searches. Below you will find some tips for each of the main searchable areas in the advanced search option:

1. **Job title** - You type the title you want to search. You can add more than one.
2. **Years of experience** (nice to have option) – You type the years or range of experience.
3. **Location** (miles option) – You type either the city or

ZIP/postal code and select the option of how many miles from that location. You can also select more than one location.

4. **Skills** (nice to have option) -You can enter skills you want to search for.

5. **Resume updated** – You can search for when the resume was last updated - from "today" to "all resumes on Monster."

6. **Diversity** (Include diversity candidate option) – You have the option to search for diversity candidates.

7. **Minimum education level** (drop down) (nice to have option) - Self-explanatory.

8. **Degree/major** (nice to have option) - You can type the major or minor you are looking for. You can add more than one.

9. **School** – You can add more than one school.

10. **Company** – You can add more than one company.

11. **Candidate's name** – Allows you to search for an actual candidate to see if they have a resume in the database.

12. **Maximum salary** (per year or per hour option) - Self-explanatory.

13. **Salary range** (drop down) - Self-explanatory.

14. **Option to include candidates without salaries** - Self-explanatory.

15. **Job type** (select option) - Self-explanatory.

16. **Job duration** (drop down) - Self-explanatory.

17. **Willing to travel** (drop down) - Self-explanatory.

18. **Relocation** (check box) – This option allows you to search for candidates who are willing to relocate.

In my experience, Power Resume Search not only gets you

better results but it also puts the best candidates at the top of the list. This saves time over executing multiple searches.

EXAMPLE OF A POWER RESUME SEARCH

Below you will find an example on how to find a Java Developer with J2SE and C++ experience who works in San Jose or New York City, as well as has banking experience and has posted their resume in the past six months.

1. **Job title** – Select multiple job title options for Java such as "engineer" or "developer."
2. **Location** (miles option) – Select "San Jose" for first location and then "New York." Also select "20 miles" as the distance of your search.
3. **Skills** – Select the options "J2SE", "Java", "C++" and "banking." Selection is required (as opposed to nice to have).
4. **Resume updated** – Select "6 months"
5. **Diversity** – Select "yes" to expand your search.

MONSTER CLASSIC RESUME SEARCH

Monster's Classic Resume Search uses Boolean, which allows users to combine keywords with operators such as "AND," "NOT" and "OR" to further produce more relevant results. There is also a selectable search option. Below you will find some tips for each of the main searchable areas in the advanced search option:

1. **Keyword** – You can use classic Boolean as well as

keywords.

2. **Resumes posted from** – You can select from "today" to "all resumes on Monster."

3. **Location options** (2 options) – a) Search by ZIP code/postal code radius or b) By state/province. It also includes an option for job seekers willing to work in the location and an option for job seekers who are authorized to work in the location.

4. **Most recent employer** - Self-explanatory.

5. **Most recent job title** - Self-explanatory.

6. **Most recent job description** – Keywords found in recent job description.

7. **School attended** - Self-explanatory.

8. **Education level** (drop down) - Self-explanatory.

9. **Career level** - Self-explanatory.

10. **Language and proficiency** - Self-explanatory.

11. **Job status** - Self-explanatory.

12. **Job types** - Self-explanatory.

13. **Company industries** – Self-explanatory.

14. **Company categories** - Self-explanatory.

EXAMPLE OF A CLASSIC RESUME SEARCH

Below you will find an example of how to find a financial advisor who works close to downtown Dallas, Texas, has a CFP, and who has applied to Monster in the past year.

1. **Keyword** – (CFP or "certified financial planner") This will pull up both CFP and certified financial planner in the search.

2. **Resumes posted from** – Select "all resumes."

3. **Location options** – Search by ZIP code "75201" and

"20 mile radius." This will pull candidates within 20 miles from downtown Dallas. Please note you will have to look up the ZIP code.

4. **Most recent job tile** – You would type "advisor."

RESUME DATABASES CONCLUSION

Paid resume databases can play an important role in finding candidates. As there is a price associated with the use of these tools, it is important that you learn how to use these tools effectively.

OPEN WEB SOURCING

For many of the hardest-to-fill roles, traditional sourcing will not be enough to find the talent you are looking for. Searching for the hardest-to-find candidates takes true Boolean skills of searching for that needle in a haystack profile. This section will focus on the Boolean open web techniques, which will help you find these candidates. The previous terms learned in the Boolean 101 section will be applied to this chapter. The best part of this section is that the candidates you find will cost nothing but internet access.

WHAT IS OPEN WEB SOURCING?

Open web sourcing is the Boolean techniques recruiters

use on search engines to find information about candidates. Information does not have to be in the form of resumes. It can take many forms, such as social media profiles, conferences lists, news articles, associations and user groups.

REALISTIC EXPECTATIONS

A very important thing to keep in mind when doing open web sourcing is the fact that when doing your searches, you will not automatically hit pay dirt and find potential candidates' profiles and information. In many cases, you will have to sift through results that are not what you are looking for until you find the info that you can use. In some instances, if you are looking for a rare profile, you might not ever find useful information. Also, after you find useful info, be aware that this is only the first step—you still might have to research contact information and then finally engage with the talent via phone/email/social media.

CREATE AN OPEN WEB GAME PLAN

The first step in doing open web sourcing is to create a game plan. Without a game plan, you can waste many hours going in the wrong direction when it comes to open web sourcing. For your game plan, you have to know what information you want to search for and the domain you want to search in. For example, you want to search on Google for actuary associations or on LinkedIn for Ruby on Rails developers user groups. Before you start your search, it is a good idea to pick about ten variations of your Boolean strings. You might only use two search strings but it is good to have this plan in case you need to rely on more than a few. Also, timing should be part of your game plan in that if you see within fifteen minutes you don't see good results, you move on to the next search strings.

BOOLEAN OPTIONS

Generally speaking, there are three ways to create Boolean strings. They are:

1. **Create your own** – This can be labor intensive, but if you know what you are doing it is easy and more customizable because you are not tied to someone else's search strings and logic. Later in this section I will give you some examples of strings to use.
2. **Use free pre-built Boolean search engines** – These are great tools as someone else has created the Boolean strings. All you need to do is to type a few keywords you are looking for and the engine does all the work for you. The one disadvantage is sometimes the Boolean strings do not cover all the areas you want to search for. Examples of some free sites to use include:
    *   Recruit'em - https://recruitin.net/ - A great site for searching for social media profiles on LinkedIn, Google+, GitHub, Xing, Stackoverflow and Twitter.
    *   TalentSonar - https://www.talentsonar.com/tools/boolean-search-generator - A great site that you can plug in information you want to search for, and it create the strings for you. The site can search on Google, Bing, and LinkedIn.

3. **Use paid pre-built Boolean search engines** – Like the free option, this is a great tool as someone else has created the Boolean for you. Two disadvantages are the cost and sometimes the Boolean strings do not cover all the areas you want to search for. I'm not giving any recommendation here, as my advice is to go with the free options.

EXAMPLES OF BOOLEAN SEARCH STRINGS

This section will give a number of examples of Boolean strings you can use for different industries, roles, and locations. The Boolean string examples will have both simple and more complex strings, and show examples of pulling different types of information such as conference attendees, associations, and profiles.

1. **Boolean search for hard-to-find candidates** - If you wanted to find a CFO with hospital experience with a CPA and not working at a home health or rehabilitation center, a simple string would be: CFO or "chief financial officer" AND CPA or "chartered professional accountant" or CPA AND (hospital or health system) NOT ("home health" and "rehabilitation").
2. **The simplest of searches** – You want to find a financial advisor. Simply type into the Google browser "find an advisor" and "directory."
3. **More complicated search by location** – If you wanted to find a Java developer in Toronto, Canada: (-job -jobs -career -opening -openings) (resume OR

cv) ("software developer" OR "software engineer" OR programmer OR "software design engineer") (near Toronto) (Java OR scala OR j2e OR jsp).

4. **Looking for members of an association** - If you wanted to look up marine engineers who belong to the International Community of Maritime and Ocean Professionals, you would search like this: site:www.sname.org (inurl:list | inurl:~members | inurl:~directory | intitle:list | intitle:~members | intitle:~directory | inurl:staff | inurl:association | inurl:board | inurl:committee | intitle:association | intitle:board | intitle:committee | intitle:staff)

5. **Looking for attendees of a conference** – If you wanted to find attendees of a pharmacy conference in New York, you would search: (list AND Pharmacy) (conference OR expo OR workshop OR seminar) (near "New York") filetype:pdf OR filetype:csv.

6. **Looking for an online resume or CV** – If you wanted to find a sales manager in Philadelphia: (resume OR CV) (Sales manager) near Philadelphia (-job -jobs -career -opening -openings) filetype:pdf OR filetype:doc.

7. **Looking for academic** – If you wanted to find a law professor in New York: Professor AND (PhD OR Ph.D) and (Law or legal) near New York.

8. **Looking for a LinkedIn Profile** - If you wanted to find a java developer in Ohio on LinkedIn: site:www.linkedin.com intitle:linkedin J2EE and Ohio -intitle:answers -intitle:updated -intitle:blog -intitle:directory -inurl:jobs.

9. **Looking for a profile on Twitter** – If you wanted to find a nurse in Dallas on Twitter: site:twitter.com

(RN OR "registered nurse") (Dallas OR Texas).

10. **Looking for a profile on Google+** - If you wanted to find an account manager in Montreal, Canada: (site:plus.google.com) (account manager) near Montreal

OPEN WEB SOURCING CONCLUSION

Learning to do open web sourcing takes both time and patience. Nonetheless, learning open web sourcing will help you find candidates that you will not find on job boards.

ADVANCED NETWORKING

One underutilized sourcing technique that many recruiters neglect is networking. The great thing about networking is that it is easy to do, it's not time consuming, and perhaps best of all, it is free.

WHAT IS RECRUITMENT NETWORKING?

Recruitment networking is a term for the techniques used by recruiters to make connections with individuals who might be good for their roles or who can refer them to potential candidates who are good for their roles.

DIFFERENT WAYS TO NETWORK

There are many ways for recruiters to network to find candidates. Below you will learn a few of these techniques:

1. **Always ask candidates for referrals** – The rule of thumb is to always ask candidates for referrals. When engaging with talent and they are not interested in your job, ask them if they know anyone who might be interested in the role. Also, candidates that you just hired are the ultimate networking gold mine. These candidates tend to be the most happy and usually are very willing to refer you talent.

2. **Network at professional social groups** – A great way to meet and network with candidates is to go to professional social groups both in person and virtually.

3. **Network with professional ethnic associations** – There are hundreds of professional ethnic associations. Many of these associations are a great place to network to spread the word about your roles.

4. **Ask the hiring manager for referrals** – Many hiring managers have connections to the very candidates you are looking to find for them. Sometimes hiring managers do not think to look in their own backyards, and by simply asking you have a quick hire.

5. **Network with other recruiters** - Some recruiters will be surprised to learn that many recruiters have no problem mutually referring talent to each other. Start building up your recruiting network connections and ask recruiters if they know anyone who would have the qualifications you are looking for.

6. **Network at professional conferences** – Attending professional conferences can be a good place to meet new connections who can potentially refer you to job seekers.

7. **Incentivize your jobs** – This one is a little controversial, but you can vastly increase your networking referral network by incentivizing your open jobs. People can be motivated when offered something tangible. Please note that when incentivizing your open jobs there can be tax issues for the receiver of the incentive. That being the case, you should get permission from your leadership and get accounting advice before implementing on your own.

8. **Do networking on social media** – Social media is a great place to network and ask for referrals.

9. **Build your personal recruitment brand** - As mentioned in the previous chapter, building your own personal brand will increase your exposure and gain new people to network and ask for referrals.

10. **Be a recruiter 24/7** – A good recruiter is always networking and looking for talent. Always keep your business cards handy when speaking with people at social gatherings. Also, always tell people that you are a recruiter and the type of people you recruit for. This could prompt people to refer you to connections.

ADVANCED NETWORKING CONCLUSION

Recruitment networking is a very simple and affordable way for recruiters to find candidates. It also should be part of all recruiter sourcing strategies.

HOW TO FIND CANDIDATES' EMAILS & PHONE NUMBERS

In many cases, when a recruiter finds a web profile on a potential candidate, it is just the first step as many web profiles do not have contact information. With no contact information available, recruiters have to come up with creative ways to find potential candidates' phone and email information.

HOW TO FIND CANDIDATES' EMAILS

Emails are one of the best ways to communicate with candidates, and not having one can make contacting a potential candidate more difficult. Learning to find emails will increase your chances of connecting with open web profiles that do not have email. Below are ways to find candidates' emails:

1. **Use websites that give you organization business email format** - These websites, which are both free and fee-based, can give you the most typical email format of organizations. After you have the format, you then add the person's name to the format and send the email out. Examples of tools include the following:
    * http://emailbreaker.com/ - free site
    * https://sites.google.com/site/

    emails4corporations/home - **free site**
-   https://emailhunter.co/ - **first 150 free**

2. **Try to figure out the email combinations yourself** - Research online and try to figure out the standard email combinations yourself.

3. **Use sites that find social media emails** - These sites give you Chrome extensions, which allows you to pick up social media profile emails. A cool tool for this is https://chrome.google.com/webstore/detail/datanyze-insider/mlholfadgbpidekmhdibonbjhdmpmafd? – **Free for now.**

4. **Try Boolean to find emails** - You can also research a potential contact's email by trying to Boolean their name with different email combinations to see if any pop up. An example of this would be to try to type their full name with quotation Jane Smith @ their business domain address. The search string would simply be: "jane smith" and "@ahss.com"

5. **Find their email in the databases you have access to** – You can also check to see if the contact has any email information in any of the databases you have access to such as your ATS/CRM, and job boards.

HOW TO FIND CANDIDATES' PHONE NUMBERS

1. **Simply look up an organization's head office number** – Basically, looking up an organization's head office number and then calling and asking to speak to the employee.

2. **Try Boolean to find phone numbers** – This only

works in some cases but is worth a quick shot. Type in the person's name, company and title into Google to see if a number pops up.

3. **Find their phone number in the databases you have access to** - You can also check to see if the contact has any phone information in any of the databases you have access to such as your ATS/CRM, and Job Boards.

4. **Use online phone directories** – If the contact does not have a common name, you can check to see if their name is listed in any online free phone directories. You will get their home phone number so you have to be comfortable calling a candidate at home.

5. **Public Records** – Search public records for names. This costs a fee to use. Also, for names that are common, it can be hard to find the person you are looking for.

7: CONCLUSION

Learning to source is an absolute fundamental skill to be a successful recruiter. Applying the sections of this chapter will hopefully bring you one step closer to that success.

8:
THE ART OF COLD CALLING

Cold calling has an important place in recruiting. For many recruiters, this is one of the hardest things to do. The ability to speak to a candidate out of the blue and convince them to be interested in a job is truly an art form. This chapter will teach recruiters how to be confident making phone calls and provide techniques to cold call into organizations.

WHY ARE COLD CALLS IMPORTANT IN RECRUITING?

If recruiters only target active job seekers, they will be overlooking the vast majority of the workforce. Depending on different stats, less than 10% of the workforce are active actively looking for jobs. That means you could potentially lose 90% of potential candidates by not cold calling.

OVERCOME YOUR COLD CALLING FEARS

For many recruiters, calling an individual out of the blue and trying to solicit them for a job is a traumatic thought. Learning to overcome these fears will make cold calling a more pleasant experience. This will translate into long-term success for you as a recruiter. Below you will find tips to overcome your cold calling fears:

1. **It's just people** – Why be scared of calling someone? Remember: the candidates you are calling are just people. They eat, sleep and make mistakes just like you, so do not be afraid of them.

2. **Always think we are doing the potential candidate a favor** – Just think that when you are cold calling, you are going to be presenting a good career opportunity to the potential candidate and doing them a favor. Logically speaking, most normal people are interested in good opportunities.

3. **Overcome rejection** - Rejection is a fact with cold calling, as only about 10% of candidates will be interested in your job. Ninety percent of candidates will not be interested so do not take it personally.

4. **Practice makes perfect** – The old saying is true. This also applies to making cold calls. The more calls you make the better and more comfortable you will be at it. My first recruitment manager made me practice cold calling over and over again. It was hard work but now it's as easy for me as riding a bike.

5. **Don't procrastinate** – Never procrastinate when making cold calls. This type of behavior will set you

up for failure, as you will be more and more hesitant to call as time goes on.

6. **Positive motivation** – Think of the reason you are making the cold calls, and that is to be successful at your job as well potential remuneration.

7. **Avoid negative thoughts** – Do not let negative thoughts betray you in terms of what can go wrong. When you make your cold calls, relax and try not to worry.

8. **Role play** – Try practicing with your colleagues, manager, and on your own. Sometimes practicing your pitch with people before talking to strangers can make you more comfortable.

9. **Have realistic expectations** – On average, only 10% of people contacted via a cold call are interested in jobs. You can never be 100% with cold calls so having realistic expectations can make you feel good.

10. **Hands on coaching** – A technique I have used with junior recruiters is to first have them listen to 3-5 of my cold calls. Then I listen to 3-5 of their calls and give them feedback. From there, they listen to 3-5 more of my cold calls. Then I listen to 3-5 more of their calls and provide more feedback. Finally, the recruiter is ready to make calls on their own. This technique helps the recruiter become comfortable.

TIPS TO CALLING INTO AN ORGANIZATION

One of the hardest things for a recruiter to do from a cold calling perspective is to call directly into an organization and ask the receptionist to put you in touch with the person you are seeking to recruit. Below are some good tips in calling into an organization:

1. **Play around with the organization's phone directory.** An easy way to bypass a company's receptionist is to play around with their phone directory. In most cases, names are easy to find and you can call them directly. You can also play around with the directory to map out org charts. At night, use the directory and listen to the employee's voicemail greeting. In many cases, the employee will list their title. If the title is someone you would be interested in, call back in the morning.

2. **Call during off-times at lunch.** Usually at lunch time, the main receptionist goes on lunch break, and the back-up will be more inclined to give you information on someone in their organization.

3. **Be direct with receptionist.** You will be surprised that if you just ask the receptionist directly to speak to a certain position in a company, they will in many cases transfer you.

4. **Learn when to abort your mission.** In some cases, a receptionist might become suspicious about you and question who you are. If you feel a call is going the wrong way, hang up and try again at another time.

5. **Block your number.** It is advisable that you block your number when making cold calls. The first reason is so the company you are calling into does not see your company's name. The second reason is so the company cannot trace you if you abort the call.

6. **When calling a lot change your voice.** If you call into the same company too often, they may start to recognize your voice. To avoid this, and it may sound funny, one option is to change the pitch and sound of your voice so they do not recognize you. An alternative is to have a colleague call in.

7. **Sound normal and not suspicious.** Try to relax and sound normal when you make cold calls. People can tell when something sounds suspicious, and will not speak with you.

STEPS TO CLOSE THE DEAL WHEN COLD CALLING

It is not good enough to merely speak with individuals when making calls. You also have to entice them to listen and take action. Below are steps to close the deal with the individuals you are cold calling:

1. Start with a quick introduction. Say your first name and company's name and then tell them you have a very interesting job opportunity. Then throw out a selling feature such as a sign-on, exciting new product to work on, or advancement.

129

2. If you see interest on their part and they are at work, ask them when is good time to speak and for a number to call, and also an email address where you may send them a job description.

3. If they are interested and have time to speak, give them more selling points on both the job and company. Follow this up by going for a quick pre-screen followed by asking them to send you their resume. Finally, ask them to fill out your company's application. My opinion is strike while the iron is hot, and you might as well go all the way if there is that much interest.

4. If they say they are not interested, ask them why not and what would interest them? Once you engage them, sometimes they reveal information that you can use to entice them.

5. If they reject you outright, ask them if they know anyone similar to themselves who could be interested in the role.

COLD CALLING CONCLUSION

By learning to make effective cold calls, you will be able to learn a skill set most recruiters are afraid of. This, in turn, will give you a valuable advantage – recruiters who make cold calls reach out to candidates that most do not contact.

9:
CANDIDATE ENGAGEMENT AND HABITS

It is not merely enough to find candidates. You have to both engage and understand candidate habits to be successful in your recruitment endeavors. This chapter will focus on providing tips and techniques to engage talent as well as to understand their habits.

CANDIDATE ENGAGEMENT

Learning how to engage talent can make the difference between success and failure in your sourcing efforts. You can contact thousands of potential candidates, but if you do not have the right messaging, those candidates will not reply to your emails/in-mails, texts and phone messages. Below you will find a list of ways to engage with candidates through emails/in-mails, texts and voice messages:

ENGAGING CANDIDATES THOUGH EMAIL/IN-MAIL

Good candidates get bombarded by recruiters every day. To stand out, you need to create emails/in-mails that will grab the candidates' attention. This section is going to be similar to the job posting section as the fundaments are the same. Here are five steps in creating an engaging email/in-mail:

STEP 1: CREATE AN EYE-CATCHING SUBJECT LINE

Candidates will make a split-second decision to open your email/in-mail based on your subject line, so create one with impact. An example might be: re: Pharmacy Manager Job with leading retailer - Interesting Job Opportunity. If you are to offer any type of sign-on bonus a title might look like this: re: ICU Registered Nurse Job - $10,000 Sign-on.

STEP 2: FIRST SECTION – EXPLAIN WHO YOU ARE AND INCLUDE A CALL TO ACTION

In a very short paragraph, briefly explain who you are, who you work for, and why the candidate's profile enticed you to email them about this great opportunity. Also, in this section you should have a call to action about next steps. It is not enough to send a great message to a candidate; you have to have a call to action and tell them the next step of replying to learn about the process. An example of might look like this:

> Hi Jane,
>
> My name is Steven Mostyn, a recruiter with Health Hospital. I saw your resume on Indeed, and it intrigued me for an ICU RN role we have open. If you are open to learning about an interesting ICU RN role with a great organization offering a $10,000 sign-on, please read the job below. If you are interested, we could set up a time to speak in more detail.

STEP 3: SECOND SECTION – TITLE, COMPANY & LOCATION

This section is self-explanatory. Briefly list the title, the company, and the location. Example of this would be:

> Position: ICU Registered Nurse
> Company: Health Hospital
> Location: Tarpon Springs, Florida

STEP 4: THIRD SECTION - SELLING THE CANDIDATE ON THE JOB/COMPANY

When looking at job descriptions, candidates have to be sold on a job in the first few sentences or they will not be interested. In many cases, these first key sentences are wasted with a long-winded description about the organization with little or no selling features. This section should be set up like the following example:

> **Top Reasons why you want to work for Health Hospital as a PCU RN:**
> - $10,000 Sign-on Bonus for qualified candidates.
> - You get to work a minute from the beach.
> - Low cost of living in one of the most affordable parts of Florida.
> - Named a Great Workplace Award winner for the seventh year in a row.
> - Warm weather and outdoor activities 12 months of the year.
> - Career growth and advancement potential

STEP 5 - FOURTH SECTION - BRIEF BUT DETAILED JOB DESCRIPTION

This section should be a detailed but brief job description. The job description should not be generic but list the actual duties about the job. An example of this section would be:

> **PCU RN Job Responsibilities:**
> - A progressive care nurse (PCU RN) works in a progressive care unit (PCU) and cares for patients who require close monitoring but do not need ICU care.
> - PCU RNs monitor cardiac and other vital information and detect any changes, thereby enabling intervention of life-threatening or emergency situations.
> - Close observation is necessary as many PCU patients receive a significant amount of complex meds, sometimes through an intravenous line that may need to be adjusted or titrated.
> - Assess, plan and evaluate patient care needs.
> - Prioritize patient care based on acuity level and available resources.
> - Assist physician during examination, treatment and procedures.
> - Administer prescribed medications, change dressings, clean wounds, monitor vital signs.
> - May expect to have a nurse/patient ratio of 1:4

OTHER EMAIL/IN-MAIL ENGAGEMENT TIPS

1. **Use standard job titles** - The job title should be a standard title that is recognizable for external candidates. If candidates do not recognize the title you use, they will not respond to your email/in-mail. For example, if your organization calls an accountant a financial advisor and that is the title you use in the job announcement that you send out, very few accountants will be interested in the job; instead you will have replies from financial planners from the investment industry.

2. **Do not have candidates directly apply to the online job application** – Most applicants prefer to speak to a recruiter before applying.

3. **Placement of text & font size** - Also important is how the text and fonts are placed to attract candidates' attention. Fonts should be large enough and easy to read but not too large or bold as to be overpowering. The text placement should be centered in such a way that the job description is visually appealing.

4. **Do not spam candidates** - Unless you are using CRM software, Indeed, or other tools that let you bypass spam, never BCC candidates. If you send emails/in-mails without using the above method, your messages will most likely wind up in a candidate's junk file.

5. **If possible use email skins** – Skins are attractive backgrounds utilizing a company's logo or other brand-specific graphics that can be placed in an email to attract a potential candidate's attention.

PUTTING IT ALL TOGETHER – CONTACTING A CANDIDATE VIA EMAIL/IN-MAIL

Below you will find a template of how the whole Email/In-mail should look to attract a candidate's attention.

Subject Line: PCU Registered Nurse Job - $10,000 Sign-on

Hi Jane,

My name is Steven Mostyn, a recruiter with Health Hospital. I saw your resume on Indeed, and it intrigued me for a PCU RN role we have open. If you are open to learning about an interesting PCU RN role with a great organization offering a $10,000 sign-on, please read the job below. If you are interested, we could set up a time to speak in more detail.

Position: PCU Registered Nurse
Company: Health Hospital
Location: Tarpon Springs, Florida

Top reasons why you want to work for Health Hospital as a PCU RN:
- $10,000 Sign-on Bonus for qualified candidates.
- You get to work a minute from the beach.
- Low cost of living in one of the most affordable parts of Florida.
- Named a Great Workplace Award winner for the seventh year in a row.
- Warm weather and outdoor activities 12 months of the year.
- Career growth and advancement potential.

PCU RN Job Responsibilities:
- A progressive care nurse (PCU RN) works in a progressive care unit (PCU) and cares for patients requiring close monitoring but do not need ICU care.
- PCU RNs monitor cardiac and other vital information and detect any changes, thereby enabling intervention of life-threatening or emergency situations.

- Close observation is necessary as many PCU patients receive a significant amount of complex meds, sometimes through an intravenous line that may need to be adjusted or titrated.
- Assesses, plans and evaluates patient care needs.
- Prioritizes patient care based on acuity level and available resources.
- Assists physician during examination, treatment and procedures.
- Administers prescribed medications, changes dressings, clean wounds, monitor vital signs.
- May expect to have a nurse/patient ratio of 1:4

Progressive Care Unit Work Hours/Shifts:
- Full Time, Days or Nights

What will you need as a PCU RN / Registered Nurse?
- Florida RN license or the ability to obtain a FL license at the time of start date.
- Basic Life Support (accredited through American Heart Association or American Red Cross)
- Experience: minimum one year of RN experience is required.

ENGAGING CANDIDATES THROUGH TEXTING

Texting candidates is becoming a more common form of communication. Learning how to engage with candidates through this medium is a must. Below you will find tips on how to engage with candidates though texting:

1. Use either a text-based app or a CRM that allows for

texting. A huge time advantage of using a CRM or a texting app is the ability to text many candidates at one time.

2. Limit your characters to under 135 characters. Texting is designed for short messages.

3. Include opt-out language so you don't anger potential candidates who do not want to be texted.

4. Make sure you spell words correctly—this is what makes you sound professional.

5. People under 45 are more likely to be receptive to texting than individuals over 45.

6. It is a good idea not to text candidates after working hours. Many candidates feel texting after hours is an intrusion on their privacy.

7. It is a good idea not to sound too aggressive in your messaging. This will turn off potential candidates.

8. Include your name, title, and company so candidates will know who you are and how to reach out to you.

9. Do not sound like an auto-generated robot. No one likes to be spammed so your language should sound like a real person.

10. Use professional language and avoid sounding casual. This is a business message.

PUTTING IT ALL TOGETHER - CONTACTING A CANDIDATE VIA TEXTING

Jane, my name is Steve. I'm a recruiter with SRM. Would you be open to an ICU role offering a $10,000 sign-on? If you want to opt out of future texts, please hit this link.

ENGAGING CANDIDATES THROUGH VOICE MESSAGES

In many cases, when reaching out to candidates via phone, you will not get a live person. That being the case, you can still leave a voice message as a form of engaging with candidates. Many recruiters do not leave voice messages. In the process, they miss a great opportunity to engage candidates with opportunities. Below you will find to create effective voice messages that will engage candidates.

STEP 1: INTRODUCTION

Your first sentence should briefly explain who you are. Mention your name, where you saw the candidate's profile, and that you have a job opportunity with the company you are recruiting for.

STEP 2: SELL THEM ON THE ROLE

Your second sentence is the most important sentence—as you have to quickly sell them on the role.

STEP 3: CALL TO ACTION

Your final sentence should tell the potential candidate how to act on the job opportunity, whether by calling you back about the job or by replying to the job description email you are going to send them.

OTHER VOICE MESSAGE TIPS

1. Keep the voice message short.
2. Sound professional and not casual.
3. Make sure to speak slowly, and ensure that your words are clear, especially when leaving your contact information.
4. Be clear who you are. If candidates understand that you are a real recruiter with a real opportunity, they will be more likely to call you back.
5. Do not sound like a used car salesman as candidates will most likely not call you back.

PUTTING IT ALL TOGETHER – EXAMPLE SCRIPT: LEAVING A VOICE MESSAGE FOR A CANDIDATE

Hi Dave, my name is Steve. I'm a recruiter with Health Hospital, and your resume on CareerBuilder intrigued me for an ER RN role I have open at our Tarpon Springs facility.

This interesting opportunity will allow you to work at Health Hospital's state-of-the art ER department. In addition, the hospital is also offering a $10,000 sign-on bonus for qualified candidates.

If this opportunity sounds appealing, please call me back at 416-111-1111. Alternatively, I sent you a detailed email. If you are interested, please let me know a good time to speak.

Thank you for your time and have a great day.

CANDIDATE HABITS

Candidate habits are always evolving. If recruiters do not keep up to date on the habits of candidates, they will not be successful in their recruiting efforts. Below are some current habits you have to understand if you want to hire more candidates:

SHORT APPLICATION PROCESS

Today's society is geared towards instant gratification. People can get instant movies and music via streaming and can order gifts from Amazon with one click. In fact, it probably took you only a few seconds to buy this book. The same social habits come into play when candidates apply for jobs. Most companies have long application processes that can take over 30 minutes to complete. Many candidates do not have the time or patience to fill out a long application without a guarantee of an interview.

Long applications are a death sentence for your candidate applicant flow; therefore, you should have short applications for your company. Below are some tips on how to have a short application process:

1. **If possible, have a quick-apply application.** The shorter you can make your application, the more likely someone will apply for your jobs.
2. **If you have to use a long application, give candidates the option to do a short or long application first.** Some companies have a longer application process due to regulatory issues. One way to get around this

is to give candidates a short application option. For short-form applications, all the candidate needs to fill in is their full name, title, company and resume. After filling out the short application, it gets email generated and sent to a recruiter. After the recruiter speaks to the candidate and gets them warmed up, the recruiter then has them apply to the long application. Speaking to the candidate first will encourage the candidate to apply; they will feel their time will not be wasted because they have already spoken with a recruiter.

3. **Take away information in the application that is not relevant.** Many job applications have information that is not relevant even from a regulatory perspective. Things to take out include: asking the same questions more than once, references, Social Security number, asking questions that require writing a sentence and, really, anything other than contact information, resume, job and education history and any compliance questions.

4. **If you use long application, make sure the resume parses.** If you have to use a long application process you should have an application process that will parse a candidate's resume. This will take all the information from the resume and it should fill in all the candidates' information about job history, education history and contact info.

5. **Use quick applies on job boards**. When posting on job boards and other media, do not send the candidate to a long application. Instead, the application should allow for a short application, which should be sent directly to the recruiter's email inbox.

MOBILE APPLICATIONS

A growing movement in job seeker behavior is many candidates applying for a job via their mobile devices. According to different statistics, anywhere between 50-70% of job seekers now apply to jobs using their mobile devices. If your application process is not mobile friendly, you could potentially lose 50-70% of job seekers. Consider these tips:

1. **Your application process has to be mobile friendly.** With most applicants applying via their mobile device, you have to ensure your application process is completely mobile friendly.
2. **Focus your paid job postings on vendors that are mobile friendly.** Job postings can be expensive. Therefore, you should use vendors whose job postings are mobile friendly.
3. **Make sure your career pages are mobile friendly.** It is one thing for your job application to be mobile friendly, but if a candidate cannot read your career page on their mobile device they likely will not apply.

CONCLUSION

To capture more candidates in your recruiting endeavors, always ensure you have engaging emails/in-mails, texts and phone messages. In addition, always keep pace with candidates' social habits and current job seeker trends such as short applications and mobile applications.

10:
INTERVIEWING AND SELECTING CANDIDATES

In order for you to submit the right candidates to your hiring managers, you have to interview and select the right candidates. This chapter will focus on how to interview candidates the right way, and how to select candidates based on those interviews.

OBJECTIVE OF A CANDIDATE INTERVIEW

The objective of a candidate interview is to determine if the candidate meets the qualifications for the roles you are working on. Another objective of candidate interviews is to make sure the candidate is a culture fit for the hiring organization. Below you will find some tips when it comes to interviewing candidates:

1. **Unless you are a domain expert, don't do a technical interview.** Many recruiters make the mistake of trying to do a technical interview when they are not an expert in that field. It is actually quite preposterous for a recruiter to make a technical assessment in something they are not an expert in.

2. **Ask basic qualifying questions.** As recruiters are most likely not domain experts, they should only ask basic qualifying questions. Your questions should focus on how many years of experience the candidate has in the major skill sets needed for the role.

3. **Do not treat the candidate like a police suspect.** When interviewing candidates, treat them with respect. Also, there is no need to be stern with candidates. Remember: you are conducting an interview, not a police interrogation. In fact, being too stern will make the candidate less interested in your roles.

4. **Use standard interview questions for the same roles you work on.** Having standard interview questions makes comparing candidates easier for both you and your hiring managers.

5. **Ask questions related to fit.** As a recruiter's job is to focus on fit, the focus of the interview should be on fit.

6. **Look for any discrepancies between a candidate's resume and what they say.** Honesty is an important thing to look for in a potential candidate. Therefore, in your interview look for any discrepancies between what the candidate says and what was reported on their resume.

7. **Do not be formal with candidates.** As you are

conducting a business job interview, do not be formal with candidates. You also want to give the impression you work for a professional organization.

8. **Close them on salary.** Part of your interview process involves closing the candidate on a salary range. You will learn more about this in chapter 12.

9. **Confirm interest after the interview.** To confirm the candidate is still interested in the role after the interview, ask them if they would be still interested in the role.

10. **Find out where they are in their job search.** To find out if the candidate is interviewing at other companies, ask them where they are in their job search. This is important in order to assess whether the candidate will be hard to close due to other job opportunities.

LIST OF STANDARD INTERVIEW QUESTIONS

1. Is the candidate eligible to work in the country you are recruiting for without any time restrictions, or are there restrictions on working for any employer?

2. Has the candidate ever interviewed or worked at the company you are representing? If yes, please provide details.

3. What is the reason the candidate is looking for a new position?

4. Ask them why they want to work for your company.

5. How many years of domain experience does the candidate have?

6. Ask the candidate to list how many years of experience they have in each of the major skill sets needed for the role.

7. Ask them about their education and certifications.

8. How many weeks of notice do they need to give their current employer before starting a new role?

9. What is the candidate's current salary, including full package, and salary expectation?

10. Ask the candidate to briefly summarize their resume. Look for discrepancies and ask them about any short stints at companies.

11. Ask the candidate a teamwork question. Ask then to tell you about a time they had to work with an uncooperative colleague. How did they work with that person, and what was the outcome?

12. Ask the candidate about a past angry client. Ask them to tell you about a time they had to deal with an angry internal or external client. Ask them the scenario and what they did to turn that relationship around.

13. If they are a manger, ask them how many years they have managed people, and the size of the teams. Also, ask them about a time they ever had to fire someone or put someone on a performance plan.

14. Ask them their short- and long-term career objectives.

15. Ask them where they are in their job search.

CANDIDATE SELECTION

After you interview a candidate for a role, you have to determine if you will select the candidate to move forward to the next step, which is typically an interview with the hiring manager. Below you will find important tips on selecting candidates:

1. **Do not be a goalie.** Hope Solo, a soccer goalie for Team USA, is a two-time gold medalist and outstanding at blocking opponents' shots on goal. As a recruiter, do not be a goalie blocking good candidates from moving forward. In recruiting, in terms of selection, as long as the candidate meets the minimum qualifications and meets the competencies of the job, you should move them forward. Many recruiters are overly critical of candidates and take potentially good candidates out of the picture.

2. **Do not submit someone who is too much of a stretch.** Recruiters sometimes like to take chances and submit candidates who are missing qualifications. There is nothing wrong with stretching on a candidate who is missing certain skill sets, but if you stretch too much your hiring manager will not be interested. In addition, if you continue to submit profiles that are not a fit, your hiring managers will no longer trust you.

3. **Never submit someone who has red flags.** If you interview a candidate and unearth red flags, do not submit them. You will only embarrass yourself—the hiring manager will also find those red flags.

4. **If you are on the fence, let the hiring manager**

decide. Sometimes when evaluating candidates, you will be on the fence. If you are not sure about something such as fit or skills, you should still present the candidate to the hiring manager and let them decide. If you were to ask any recruiter how many times over the years they have submitted three candidates and the one they thought was the third choice was hired and their first choice was rejected, they probably would say "too many times."

CONCLUSION

If a recruiter does his or her job properly and evaluates candidates based on qualifications and culture fit for a role, the hiring manager should end up with talented people to consider.

11:
FAST HIRING PROCESS

If you recruit for hard-to-fill roles, it is absolutely necessary that you have a fast hiring process. In this chapter, we will discuss the importance of having a fast hiring process and how to get proper candidate feedback from your hiring managers.

THE IMPORTANCE OF HAVING A FAST HIRING PROCESS

In any hard-to-fill recruitment space, it is absolutely a candidates' market, where candidates can pick and choose where they want to go. If you can actually find a viable candidate for your hard-to-fill roles and your hiring process takes too many days, you will lose your candidate. All those hours it took you to screen and interview that candidate can be lost in an instant due to a slow hiring process.

The longer a candidate is on the job market, the greater the chance that her or she is going to receive a job offer. As a result, the longer it takes to get a candidate through your interview and selection process, the higher the likelihood that you are going to lose that candidate to a competitor. It is of the upmost importance you learn how to have a fast hiring process.

YOUR HIRING LIFE CYCLE SHOULD BE ONLY FIVE DAYS!

This might shock many recruiters, but the perfect life cycle for filling hard-to-fill roles should only be five business days from the time you submit your candidate to your hiring managers.

If you can get your candidates through a recruiting life cycle in only five business days, you will turn a higher percentage of qualified candidates into hires. You will also beat out your competitors, which will give you a competitive edge in the market.

STEPS TO GETTING YOUR HIRING LIFE CYCLE DOWN TO ONLY FIVE DAYS

DAY 1 - INTERVIEW AND SUBMIT YOUR CANDIDATE.

The same day you interview your candidate, submit him or her to your hiring manager for review or set up an interview on your hiring manager's calendar for an interview.

DAY 2 (OPTIONAL STAGE) HIRING MANAGER REVIEWS RESUME.

24 hours after you submit the candidate to the hiring manager, the hiring manager has to let you know if they want to move forward and set up an interview immediately. In your process, you can even skip this stage if you develop a relationship with your hiring manager to set up interview directly on the manager's calendar.

DAYS 2-4 – HIRING MANGER INTERVIEWS YOUR CANDIDATE AND MAKES AN OFFER.

24-72 hours after the hiring manager reviews the candidate, the manager should interview your candidate. Alternatively, if you put the interview on your hiring manager's calendar, you should do so 24-72 hours after you interview the candidate.

Also, as soon as the hiring manager finishes interviewing the candidate, the manager needs to decide if an offer will be made. You might be thinking: how it is possible for a hiring manager to interview and make an offer to a candidate 24-72 hours after you interview the candidate or the hiring manager reviews the resume? The answer to this is: you have to develop relationships with your hiring managers. You will learn strategies later in this chapter on how to get your hiring manager to move faster, including interviewing right away.

DAYS 2-5 – MAKE OFFER TO THE CANDIDATE THE SAME DAY THE HIRING MANAGER DECIDES TO MAKE AN OFFER.

After the candidate interviews and the hiring manager decides to make an offer, immediately make the offer to the candidate.

HOW TO GET BUY-IN ON A FAST HIRING PROCESS

One of the biggest barriers in moving candidates through the recruitment process is not getting feedback on submitted or interviewed candidates. To overcome that barrier, you must learn how to be a recruitment business partner with your hiring managers and other stakeholders. Below you will learn how to develop relationships with your stakeholders in order to get buy-in on a fast hiring process.

EDUCATE STAKEHOLDER ON THE ADVANTAGES OF A FAST-HIRING PROCESS.

For most normal organizations, hiring key talent is fundamental to the growth of that organization. Many leaders understand that not hiring talent can lead to stagnant growth. Part of your job is to educate them about the importance of creating SLAs (service level agreements) on a fast-hiring process. Below you will find out how to educate stakeholders on a fast hiring process and how to get buy-in:

1. **Educate whoever has representation with your executive suite.** Depending on the organization you work for or on behalf of, different people will have relationships with the executive suite. For smaller or mid-sized companies, that could be you as the recruiter or an HR leader/recruitment manager. For larger organizations, that could be a director/VP of HR or the director/VP of recruitment. In order to educate the representative of your executive suite, you need to educate them on the advantages of a having a fast hiring process. The first step is to set up a meeting and create a presentation. Your presentation will include analytical information about how many days it takes to move a candidate through the process and how many candidates you are losing. The presentation should show that having a faster hiring process with SLAs will result in more hires for hard-to-fill roles and, therefore, save your company revenue. It might take you a few attempts, but if you can prove the net gain of a fast hiring process most normal leaders will have buy-in.

2. **Educate executives.** After you get buy-in from the representative who deals with the executive suite, they need to educate the executives on the fast hiring process. Using the same analytics and presentation that was done previously, the executives should be shown the data that supports having a fast hiring process. Most smart leaders will accept the

recommendation and allow you to move forward with a fast hiring process.

EDUCATE HIRING MANAGERS ON NEW FAST HIRING PROCESS SLA

It is not merely enough to have executive buy-in on a fast hiring process; you still need your hiring manager's buy-in as well. After the executives have approved the SLA for a fast hiring process, you need to educate and get support from your hiring managers. It is recommended that you set up individual meetings with your hiring managers. At these meetings, educate them on why the new fast hiring process will help ensure they receive the talent they need to run their business. Also, educate them on the fact that the fast hiring process will ensure they hire the needed hard-to-fill candidates before their competitors have a chance to do so. Most smart hiring managers do not want to lose candidates to their competitors and are very willing to work with the fast hiring process.

CONCLUSION

It may take both time and effort to achieve a fast hiring process, but by doing so you will set yourself up for success as a recruiter.

12:
CLOSING CANDIDATES

Closing candidates is an art form and usually the last step in the recruitment process. This occurs after your candidate gets an offer and you close them to accept and join the organization you represent. If this is not done correctly, all of your hard work up to this point can be lost.

CLOSING RATE PERCENTAGES

According to most experts, your closing rates should be close to 90 percent of all candidates who receive an offer. If your closing rate is not at this level, there are ways to improve your closing techniques. If candidates do not accept your offers, it's important to understand why. Below you will learn techniques to improve your closing rate as well as how to overcome closing stumbling blocks:

TIPS TO IMPROVE YOUR CLOSING TECHNIQUES

1. **Always pre-close candidates.** It is very important, from the first conversation you have with your candidate, to understand his or her current salary package and what the candidate is looking for in terms of total salary. If you know this information, there will be less surprises at the closing stage. Simply put, if the candidate is asking for a salary that is well beyond your organization's pay structure, then there is a very high chance that the organization will not be able to meet that demand. If you cannot afford the candidate's required salary, it is better to save your time and the candidate's time by ending the conversation at the first interview.

2. **Besides salary, you should know what other benefits the candidate wants.** Find out how many days of vacation, benefits, and any other tangible requests the candidate has. If there is anything the candidate absolutely needs that your organization cannot offer, there is a good chance the candidate will not accept.

3. **Sell them on what they want.** During the interview process, a good recruiter will find out what the candidate wants and why they are looking for a job. During the offer process, bring up things they want like the particular role, location, or other key benefits.

4. **Many candidates always ask for more.** Candidates will always ask for top dollar but in most cases will accept less than their stated demands.

5. **In situations where an offer is less than what a candidate expects,** you can sell candidates on things like bonuses, hourly differentials, promotional potential, location, and company culture.

6. **Do not be afraid to negotiate.** If an offer comes in that is less than what the candidate wants, do not let this be the end of the conversation. In many cases, what the candidate wants and what is offered do not match. This is where your closing skills are needed. In many cases, you can bring the candidate down in their salary demands and in some cases you can get more money or perks from your company, especially for real hard-to-fill roles.

7. **Provide extra customer service to your candidates.** Developing your relationship with your client through extra customer service will make closing much easier. If your candidate trusts you throughout your relationship, they will be more likely to take your offer over other recruiters' offers.

HOW TO IMPROVE CLOSING STUMBLING BLOCKS

There will be times when it does not matter how good of a closer you are. Some candidates will not accept due to various stumbling blocks. Below are some of these stumbling blocks and some solutions to solve these issues so you can close candidates:

1. **The salary is way below market value.** If your

salaries are way below market rate, you will have a very difficult time closing candidates. To get your salaries at market level, you need to convince whoever handles salary that levels must change. Be it finance, executive level or compensation, you need to show them data that supports your claim. One tip is to show them data on how many offers were lost due to compensation being low. A second tip is to show them stats about salary levels in the industry. For this, you can work with compensation to do a salary survey. You can also use outside vendors to research your competitors to prove you have low salaries.

2. **The hiring manager did not do a good selling job to the candidate.** You might have situations where a hiring manager does a poor job interviewing. In this case, you have to educate that hiring manager to do a better job selling their roles to the candidate.

3. **Recent negative publicity about the organization you represent.** For different reasons, an organization might receive short-term or even long-term negative publicity. This can greatly impact your ability to close candidates, especially when the negative publicity has happened recently. This is one of the most difficult situations to overcome. The best way to deal with this situation is to sell the candidate on the current positives. A good example is a company that has had recent management changes. You can spin this as a good time to come in and grow and advance as the company rebuilds.

4. **Better counteroffer.** Nothing can frustrate a recruiter more than a candidate taking a counteroffer with their current company. Sometimes there is nothing

you can do, as you might have been played by the candidate who used your offer to get a better offer with their current firm. In some cases, you can go back to the candidate and explain logically that if they accept the counteroffer with their current company they will not be trusted anymore for having tested the job market.

5. **Better offer somewhere else.** You could have done everything right in terms of closing a candidate, but if they get a better offer it will be very hard to close the deal. The only thing you can try to do is offer something to the candidate that the other offer does not have: more career growth, other benefits such as more vacation days, work flexibility or something else that can sell the candidate on the role.

THE CLOSE IS NOT THE END

Even if you close a candidate, they still might not show up for work. It is important that you stay in touch with the candidate all the way to their start date. By staying in touch with the candidate, you can find out if there are any misgivings about starting. You can also confirm that they gave in their notice. In addition, the candidate will appreciate the extra service of you checking up on them.

CONCLUSION

By learning the art of closing candidates, you will ensure all your hard work is not lost at the offer stage.

13:
THE CLIENT AND CANDIDATE EXPERIENCE

A much-neglected area of recruitment is the client and candidate experience. By developing this neglected area, a recruiter will improve his or her long-term relationships with both hiring managers and candidates.

WHAT IS THE CLIENT & CANDIDATE EXPERIENCE?

The client and candidate experience is the positive emotional experiences you leave with both your hiring managers and candidates through your interactions with them as a recruiter.

THE IMPORTANCE OF THE CLIENT & CANDIDATE EXPERIENCE

How many times have you given your business to someone based solely on customer service? In some cases, you will even pay more for something due to the customer service you receive. The same thing applies to recruitment. Providing extra customer service to your candidates can be the difference between the candidate signing with your organization or going somewhere else. This also applies to your hiring managers; providing extra customer service enhances your relationships and trust levels. This will allow you to work more effectively with your hiring managers, and as a result hire more candidates.

HOW TO IMPROVE YOUR CUSTOMER SERVICE WITH YOUR HIRING MANAGERS

Improving your customer service with your hiring managers is not a hard task to accomplish. Although it is not a hard task, it can make a huge difference in the success of your relationship. Below are some great tips to improving your customer service with your hiring managers:

1. **Be reliable** – This is one of the best ways to provide customer service to your hiring managers. If you are always reliable, your hiring managers will see your value and will trust working with you.

2. **Get hires** – This is the most obvious way to develop trust with your hiring managers. If managers see you can deliver, they will begin to trust you.

3. **Do not delay contacting candidates** – Hiring managers hate when candidates are not contacted quickly.

4. **Make quick offers** – Nothing will tick off a hiring manager more than delaying or losing a candidate at the offer stage.

5. **Be honest** – Hiring managers would rather you be honest with them than blow smoke about something you do not know or cannot do.

6. **Always return the calls, texts, and emails of your managers** – Managers want to feel important; therefore, without exception, always return your hiring managers phone calls, emails and texts.

7. **Always be available for your managers via many forms of communication such as phone, email, text and instant messenger.** Making yourself available via more than one form of communication will earn credibility with your hiring managers.

8. **Go the extra mile for your hiring managers** – This can go a long way. An example of an extra thing you can do for your hiring manager is to provide market intelligence.

9. **After hires are made, send thank-you emails** – Make sure your managers know how much you value their partnership.

10. **Under-promise and over-deliver** – Never promise something you cannot deliver. Instead over-deliver and your hiring managers will be eating out of your hands.

HOW TO IMPROVE YOUR CUSTOMER SERVICE WITH YOUR CANDIDATES

Some recruiters fail to provide great customer service to their candidates. This is a huge mistake. Below you will find key ways to improve your customer service with your candidates. Some of these things are similar to the customer service you build with your hiring managers.

1. **Always return the calls, texts, and emails of candidates.** Candidates always want to feel important. Return your candidates' phone calls, emails and texts promptly.

2. **Never brush anyone off.** A candidate might not be a fit today, but they might be the perfect one later on. These candidates can also be a great resource for referrals.

3. **Always provide feedback right away after an interview or submission.** Not getting back to a candidate following an interview or submission is a huge mistake. Many candidates just want to know where they stand, and a simple email can provide them with needed closure.

4. **Give offers right away.** Make offers to your candidates right away as this will show the candidate you are committed to helping them.

5. **Be honest.** Candidates would rather you be honest with them than blow smoke about something you do not know or cannot do.

6. **Give them career advice and resume tips.** I have placed many candidates over the years who at first

were not interested in jobs I was recruiting for. By providing customer service on something the candidate needed, they became a loyal candidate who I placed. Things you can provide for candidates include market intelligence, career advice, and resume tips.

7. **Send thank-you emails, phone calls, or texts.** Everyone likes to be appreciated, and sending a thank-you note to a candidate you spoke with can go a long way in showing your appreciation.

CONCLUSION

Providing exceptional customer service to your hiring managers and your candidates does not take much effort, but having happier hiring managers and candidates will result in more success for you as a recruiter.

14:
DATA-DRIVEN RESULTS

An area of recruitment that has a tremendous impact on improving performance is data-driven recruitment analytics. How do recruiters truly know how they are performing? How does an individual recruiter get better? How are the tools performing? These questions and many others can be answered by analytics. This chapter will focus on analytics, discuss some of the more important metrics, how to use metrics to make better decisions, and look into the future of analytics.

WHAT IS RECRUITMENT ANALYTICS?

Recruitment analytics is where a recruitment function takes current and past recruitment data to determine performance to make better recruitment decisions going forward.

IMPORTANT RECRUITMENT METRICS

There are many different recruitment metrics you can report on. Knowing what metrics to focus on is important. You want to focus on metrics that will improve a recruiter's performance. Below you will find some of the more common metrics:

RECRUITMENT LIFE CYCLE METRICS

Recruitment life cycle metrics are the stats that let you know how fast a recruiter and hiring manager are moving in the recruitment life cycle. Below are the major stats in this category:

1. **Days to contact applying candidates.** This stat tells you how many days it takes a recruiter to contact applicants. For this stat, a recruiter consistently should contact in less than 24 hours. On average, 80 percent of candidates lose interest when not called right away.
2. **Days to submit after screen stage.** This stat tells you how many days it takes a recruiter to submit a candidate after being screened. For this stat, a recruiter should be at less than 24 hours in order to have a fast hiring process.
3. **Days for hiring manager to review.** If you have a review stage, this stat will tell you how many days a hiring manager is taking to review candidates. In order to have a fast hiring process, the review stage should be less than 24 hours.

4. **Days for hiring manager to interview.** This stat will tell you how many days it takes a hiring manager to interview submitted or reviewed candidates. In order not to lose candidates, this stat should be no longer than 72 hours.

5. **Days to make offers after interview.** This stat tells you how many days it takes a hiring manager to make an offer after an interview. It should be less than 24 hours.

6. **Days for candidates to receive an offer.** This stat tells you how many days it takes a hiring manager to make an offer after an interview. It should be less than 24 hours.

7. **Time to Fill.** This is the most common stat in recruitment. This stat tells you how many days it takes to fill a role from the time it is posted until you close the requisition. This stat will vary from industry to industry and the difficulty of the role to fill. The average for non-hard-to-fill is 30 days and for hard-to-fill, 60 days. For the rarest of skill sets, this stat could be over one year.

SOURCING METRICS

Sourcing metrics are the stats that tell you how well an organization is sourcing candidates as well as how well sourcing tools are performing and at what cost.

1. **Contact to submission ratio** - This metric measures

how many contacts it takes to get a candidate interested in the role you are sourcing for. This important stat will show how successful a recruiter's solicitation communication is with the candidates through calls, emails, in-mails, and texts. The industry average for contact to interest ratio is 25%. So if a recruiter contacts 100 candidates, 25 should be interested in the role. One way to improve this statistic is for recruiters to improve their engagement with candidates through phone, email, in-mail and texting.

2. **Hours to submission ratio** - This metric calculates how many hours it takes for a recruiter to get a submission. This metric is important as it lets a sourcer know if he or she is working too many hours to get a submission. This stat changes from industry to industry, but the industry average to get a submission for hard-to-fill roles is eight hours, according to leading recruitment analytical expert David Szary of Lean Human Capital. For this stat, the sourcer calculates the number of submissions completed in the core sourcing hours worked over a month's period. For example, if a sourcer worked 160 hours and only 100 of those hours were spent sourcing, then the sourcer would only factor 100 hours into the equation. The core sourcing hours worked (100) would then be divided by the sourcer's submissions for that month. The final equation would look like: 100 core sourcing hours worked ÷ 25 monthly submissions = 4 hours worked to get a submission.

3. **Submission to interview ratio** - This metric

determines how many direct-sourced submitted candidates it takes to get an interview. The metric can give an indication of the quality of the submission. The industry average is 75%. If a recruiter fails to get at least 75% of submitted candidates to the interview stage, it is recommended that a recruiter look at the quality of their submissions. A suggestion to help improve this statistic is: doing more in-depth intakes with hiring managers to better understand their needs. Another tip is to develop stronger relationships with hiring managers in order to sell them on candidates.

4. **Interview to offer ratio** – This metric determines how many candidate interviews it takes to get an offer. The industry average is three interviewed candidates to get an offer. One suggestion for improving this statistic is to better screen candidates who meet the hiring manager's criteria. Another good tip is to speak with the hiring manager after the interview to find out on a micro-level what candidates are missing in terms of soft skills and technical skills. By adjusting based on the hiring manager's feedback, you will improve this stat.

5. **Offer to acceptance ratio** - This metric looks at the percentage of offers accepted by candidates. The industry average is 90%. To improve this stat, do a better job of closing or working with your hiring managers on removing barriers (such as low salary).

6. **Source of hire** - The source of hire is the sources (paid and free) where all of your hires come from. This important stat lets you know what tools are producing the most hires and where to spend your

time and money in terms of recruitment tools.

7. **Cost per hire (ROI of hire)** – Sourcing tools can be quite expensive, and investing in the right tools can make or break a recruitment team. It is paramount that every recruitment department take inventory of where its hires come from and the cost per hire of every direct-source hire. This information is powerful – it will tell you where to invest or divest. Sometimes the analytics can be surprising. For example, a source may generate hires but the cost per hire of that source may be more than an agency fee. The ROI on a great tool should be under $1,000 per hire. If it is an average tool, the ROI is under $2,000 per hire, while anything over $3,000 per hire is a poor performing tool that you should divest from. The best and most accurate way to collect the source of a sourced hire is to track source tags in a CRM. If a recruiting team does not have a CRM, then an SLA should be created that specifies that recruiters manually track the sources of their hires. Collecting ROI is very simple: just calculate the cost of a tool divided by how many direct-sourced hires you have from that source. For example, if a tool costs $100,000 and you have 200 hires, then your ROI equation would look like this: $100,000 \div 200 = \$500$ cost per hire.

SUPPLY AND LABOR DEMAND STATS

Another important analytical area for a recruiter to

understand is supply and labor demand stats. These stats allow a recruiter to make informed decisions in terms of how to recruit based on supply and demand, and also how to give hiring managers realities for the market. Below you will learn about wanted analytics, which is a useful tool in this space.

Wanted analytics – This is a great tool that helps recruiters determine the supply and labor demand for the market and locations they recruit for. Wanted analytics take both national labor stats and national job board stats and create real time stats that can show you how hard it will be to recruit for a particular role, as well as the supply of that role.

THE FUTURE OF RECRUITMENT ANALYTICS

For many years, recruitment was far behind many professions in terms of metrics. Most recruiters today are still behind the times and only look at their internal performance with no real thought about what's happening externally. With the advent of national recruitment industry benchmarking, this has changed over the past few years. This type of benchmarking can let a recruitment department know how it is performing nationally compared to its peers in the industry from a recruitment perspective. Below you will find two organizations who are doing a great job in this space.

- **Lean Human Capital** – http://www.leanhumancapital. com/recruitx.php This is the top recruitment analytical company, with an emphasis on health care. Over the years, Lean Human Capital has taken data from many health care organizations to determine national benchmarking standards for recruitment departments. Lean Human Capital can analyze data from an organization to determine how well that organization is performing compared to its peers.

- **ERE Talent Acquisition Benchmarking** – http://info.eremedia.com/benchmarking/ This is another great place to get national benchmarking to determine how well a recruitment department is performing compared to its peers. ERE's talent acquisition benchmarking provides the most accurate and actionable performance metrics ever available, based on raw data and hard facts, not opinions or surveys. With millions of data points from a large set of diverse companies, it provides valuable insights into industry metrics regarding speed, quality and more.

CONCLUSION

By using analytics as part of your overall recruitment strategy, you can learn how you are preforming as a recruiter, how to improve, and better understand how your sourcing tools are performing.

15:
NEVER STOP LEARNING

Recruitment is an ever-evolving discipline. Whoever does not change with the times becomes a dinosaur. When I first started recruiting, we had no job boards. Resumes were faxed and mailed. If I would have stuck to this style of recruitment, I would not be employed right now and I certainly would not have written this book. I've always tried to embrace the latest advances in technology. In fact, when the first major job board, Monster, came out, most of my co-workers thought I was wasting my time with this new tool. Six months later, I had surpassed all of my colleagues who failed to adapt to this innovation.

Without continuing to learn new tools, techniques and best practices, a recruiter will eventually stop moving forward; therefore, it is of the upmost importance that recruiters never stop learning.

This chapter focuses on great resources to continue your learning. Also, please note that although I have written for ERE Media, Lean Human Capital and Recruiting Headlines, I am not a paid employee and therefore can make my recommendations without any paid bias.

RECRUITER ONLINE MAGAZINES

The following online recruitment magazines are recommended for learning and growing your recruitment skills:

- **ERE Media** – http://www.eremedia.com/ ERE Media is the most well-known and largest recruitment-specific news site on the web, with over 200,000 unique visitors per month. The site has three areas where they produce useful and advanced articles, including SourceCon, TLNT, and ERE. Below you will learn about each of them

- **SourceCon** - http://www.eremedia.com/sourcecon/ SourceCon is the leading and most well-known site on the web for sourcing news and tips. I have personally written for this magazine and you can find my author's page here: http://www.eremedia.com/author/steven-mostyn/

- **TLNT** - http://www.eremedia.com/tlnt/ TLNT provides news, opinions, and analysis for HR leaders, talent management leaders, and professionals.

- **ERE** - http://www.eremedia.com/ere/ ERE provides news and tips for recruiters and talent acquisition professionals.

- **Recruiting Headlines** - http://recruitingheadlines.com/ This is another great site with original content, and also contains recruitment news that has been aggregated from across the web.

CONVENTIONS

The following convention is recommended as a great place to learn from experts and to network with your peers:

- **SourceCon** - http://www.eremedia.com/events/ At SourceCon, recruiters have the chance not only to learn from world-class sourcing practitioners but also to interact with some of the brightest minds in sourcing. During breakout sessions, there is always a heavy stream of new and innovative sourcing ideas being exchanged by sourcers from around the world.

VENDOR-PROVIDED TRAINING

Never take for granted that most sourcing vendors will provide great training and support of their products. Vendors are smart enough to know that if you use their products more effectively and get more results, you will most likely keep their products. Also, more likely than not, the vendors will give you new insight into using their products. Best of all, the cost of vendor-provided training is almost always the best price of all: free!

WEBINARS

Webinars are a great place for recruitment learning which can be done in the convenience of your home or office. Below you will find some recommended webinars:

- **Lean Human Capital** - http://www.leanhumancapital.com/events.php. Listen to some of the industry thought leaders, as well analytical and training guru Dave Szary, give great information on recruitment tips on such topics as: analytics, sourcing, recruitment marketing, and many more.
- **ERE** - http://www.eremedia.com/webinars/ Leading recruitment and sourcing thought leaders speak on some great webinars here.

RECRUITMENT TRAINING & CERTIFICATIONS

There are many recruitment training courses and certifications available. The best recruitment certification course I would recommend is the Recruiter Academy run by Lean Human Capital (http://www.recruiteracademy.com/training/certified-recruiter-program/). This online or in-person program is a great way for recruiters to develop their whole recruitment game, as well as to improve their time management skills. After completing the training, recruiters receive either the Certified Recruiter or Certified Mentor certification.

TRAINING BY ME, AUTHOR STEVEN MOSTYN

I regularly appear in the media and give presentations or speak about recruitment and sourcing, so follow me on social media to find my latest articles, books, webinars, seminars and training programs. Follow me on: LinkedIn (https://www. linkedin.com/in/stevenmostyn); Facebook (https://www. facebook.com/stevenmostynmba/) and Twitter (https://twitter. com/top_headhunter.).

CONCLUSION

By continuing to learn as a recruiter, you will stay relevant with your craft and be able to have a long and successful career.

CONCLUSION

To find true success in the recruitment industry, you have to understand the basic fundamentals of your trade. By mastering the 15 fundamentals explained in this book, you can achieve your goal of becoming a great recruiter.

If you have any questions, feel free to communicate with me via email at steven.mostyn@yahoo.com or on social media: https://www.linkedin.com/in/stevenmostyn; https://www.facebook.com/stevenmostynmba/ and https://twitter.com/top_headhunter

THANK YOU

I want to thank the following individuals for their long-term support and for helping making this book possible:

Korinne Carpino, my current manager, for her continued support.

My HR leaders at Adventist Health System: Akbar Sultan and Olesea Azevedo.

My current staff at Adventist Health System.

David Szary of Lean Human Capital.

My book editor & formatter, Melissa Bailey

The following industry innovators for their support over the years: Greg Arbitman, Frances Arthur, Gail Atlas, John Bennett, Candice Bergermann, Jeff Chaitoff, Julie Cober, Donna Corsano, Rene Elhadad, Harold Ensley, Estrella Frias, Sonja Gay, Allan Gosyne, Kevin Hamann, Nikki Kemp, Davis Kim, Olga Larionova, Tim Lawlor, May Lo, Laurent Longin, Colin Lyle, Sharon Mararac, Steven Murray, Rob Navarrete, Nicole Nespeca, Ted Pierni, Shannon Pritchett, Sarah Rutherford, Emma Scott, Patty Simmons, Liza Voticky, Melissa Wallace, Susan Wilson, Melissa Woodley, and Debra Yarnall.

My close friends Dave, Lee, Mark, Nachum, Nicole, Sonja, Suzan, Rick and Ryan.

My Uncle Alan and Aunt Sheila, and my Uncle Brian.

My in-laws, Bea & Ronnie Rocklin, and my sisters-in-law Rochel and Shaindy.

My brother Shawn, who has always been there for me.

My father Murray Mostyn, for being such great role model.

My mom, who was my guiding light.

My children Jonah, Kayla, Daniel, and Elijah, for being my inspiration.

Finally, my wife Sarah, without whom I am nothing.

GLOSSARY

ATS: Acronym for applicant tracking system. ATSs are systems designed to store, track, audit, and move candidates through the whole recruiting life cycle.

Backpage: http://www.backpage.com/ A free classified site where you can post jobs.

Bing: https://www.bing.com/A large search engine owned by Microsoft. It has a steady flow of users due to the number of consumers who use Microsoft's Internet Explorer browser, which promotes Bing as a search engine.

Boolean: Sequences of word commands used in databases or search engines to find information.

Candidate Interview: The objective of a candidate interview is to determine if the candidate meets the qualifications for the roles you are working on as well to make sure the candidate is a culture fit for your organization.

CareerBuilder: http://www.careerbuilder.com/ One of the longest-running job boards. It has a loyal following among some job seekers.

Client and Candidate Experience: The positive emotional experiences you leave with both your hiring managers and candidates through your interactions with them as a recruiter

Craigslist: https://www.craigslist.org/about/sites The most well-known online classified site. The site is free to post jobs in smaller locations.

CRM: Acronym for customer relationship management. CRMs are systems designed to store and track candidates. These systems are usually better at searching and making contact with candidates than ATSs.

Closing candidates: The usual last step in the recruitment process. After your candidate gets an offer, you close with them when he or she accepts and joins the organization you represent.

Directory Books: These mostly paid services were the forerunner of the internet. Directory books list key people in specific professions.

Domain knowledge: The important business intelligence you need to know about the industry you recruit in, your client or organization, and the roles you recruit for.

Facebook: https://www.facebook.com/ The largest social media site with over 1.65 billion active users and growing.

DuckDuckGo: https://duckduckgo.com/ A fast growing

search engine that some consumers prefer because it protects searchers' privacy.

ERE Media: http://www.eremedia.com/ ERE Media is the most well-known and largest recruitment-specific news site on the web, with over 200,000 unique visitors per month. The site has three areas where they produce useful and advanced articles: SourceCon, TLNT and ERE.

ERE's Talent Acquisition Benchmarking: Provides the most accurate and actionable performance metrics available based on raw data and hard facts, not opinions or surveys. With millions of data points from a large set of diverse companies, it provides valuable insights into industry metrics regarding speed, quality and more.

Glassdoor: https://www.glassdoor.com/index.htm The top employee review website where current and past employees give reviews about their experiences working at their organization.

Google: https://www.google.com/ The largest and most well-known search engine in the world.

Google AdWords: Google's advertising platform, where you can pay to have a higher ranking on Google.

Hire Up: http://www.gogohireup.com/post-jobs-for-free A free job site specializing in technology.

Indeed: http://www.indeed.com/ The largest job board

site with over 180 million unique visitors each month and growing. Indeed is different than any other job board as it works more like a search engine than a traditional job board.

Intake session: A detailed meeting you have with your hiring managers where you learn important information about the requisition you are assigned to. Intake sessions are essential in order to understand the true needs of your external and internal clients. These are a must to successfully fill a role.

Job Aggregators: Job board search engines that collect job posting across the internet and make them easily searchable.

Job Spider: http://www.jobspider.com/ A classified site where you can post jobs for free.

Juju: https://www.juju.com A Job aggregator.

Lean Human Capital: http://www.leanhumancapital. com/ The top recruitment analytical company with an emphasis on health care. Lean Human Capital has taken data from many health care organizations to determine national benchmarking standards for recruitment departments. Lean Human Capital can analyze data from any organization to determine how well that organization is performing compared to its peers.

LinkedIn: https://www.linkedin.com/ The world's largest

professional social media site with over 433 million active users.

Monster: http://www.monster.com/ One of the original career sites with a loyal following.

Needjobsoon: http://www.needjobsoon.com/employer A free job posting site.

Oodle: http://www.oodle.com/ A free classified job posting site.

Open Web Sourcing: The Boolean techniques used by recruiters on search engines to find information about candidates. Information does not have to be in the form of resumes; it can take many forms such as social media profiles, conferences lists, news articles, associations and user groups.

Paid Online Directories: These sites can provide information on professionals you are looking for. Examples of these sites include ZoomInfo, Data.com, and Hoovers.

Personal Recruitment Brand: The way in which recruiters create awareness and information around themselves as a recruiter.

Post Jobs for Free: http://www.postjobfree.com/ A free job aggregator.

Recruiter Academy: http://www.recruiteracademy.com/

training/certified-recruiter-program/ This online or in-person program is a great way for recruiters to develop their whole recruitment game as well as to improve time-management skills. After completing the training, recruiters receive either a Certified Recruiter or Certified Mentor certification.

Recruit'em: https://recruitin.net/ A great site for searching for social media profiles on LinkedIn, Google+, GitHub, Xing, Stackoverflow and Twitter. The site is great as it creates the Boolean search strings for you.

Recruitment Analytics: Where a recruitment function abstracts current and past recruitment data to determine performance in order to make better recruitment decisions going forward.

Recruitment Branding: The art of creating a corporate presence for candidates so that they will recognize your brand and be interested in becoming employees of that brand.

Recruiting Headlines: http://recruitingheadlines.com/ A recruitment news site with original content and recruitment news that has been aggregated from across the web.

Recruitment Life Cycle: The different phases a candidate goes through in the recruitment and hiring process.

Recruitment Life Cycle Metrics: The stats that let you know how fast a recruiter and hiring manager are moving in the recruitment life cycle.

Recruitment Networking: The techniques used by recruiters to make connections with individuals who might be good for their roles or for referring potential candidates who are good for their roles.

Return on Time (ROT), from a sourcing perspective: The art of how to improve your sourcing speed through a set of steps that ensures your time is focused on techniques and tools that maximize your sourcing time. This technique was created by the author of this book.

Search Engine Optimization (SEO): The methods used to increase the amount of people who visit a website by obtaining a high-ranking placement in the search results page of a search engine or job board.

SourceCon: http://www.eremedia.com/events/ SourceCon is the most well-known sourcing convention in the world where recruiters have the chance to learn from world-class sourcing practitioners and interact with some of the brightest minds in sourcing.

Speed Sourcing: The techniques and tools used to find and attract candidates quicker.

Sourcing: The art of finding and attracting candidates through a multitude of innovative techniques.

Sourcing metrics: The stats that tell you how well an

organization is sourcing candidates. Provides feedback on how well sourcing tools are performing and at what cost.

Stackjobs: https://stackjobs.co.uk/ A free UK-focused job posting site.

Steven Mostyn: Author of *Recruiting 101: The Fundamentals of Being a Great Recruiter.*

Talent Mapping: This is where you call into an organization to map out the key people you are looking to recruit.

TalentSonar: https://www.talentsonar.com/tools/boolean-search-generator A great site that you can plug in information that you want to search for, and it creates the strings for you. The site can search on Google, Bing, and LinkedIn.

The Ladders: https://recruit.theladders.com/ A site that specializes in posting management roles.

Trovit: https://www.trovit.com/ A free classified job posting site.

Twitter: https://twitter.com/ A social media site where users can send out short messages. The site is very popular among celebrities and has over 300 million active users.

US.jobs: http://us.jobs/indexingrequest.asp A federal government site where you can post jobs for free.

Veterans Employment Center: https://www.vets.gov/employment/employers/ This site allows you to post jobs for Veterans.

Wanted Analytics: A great tool that help recruiters determine the supply and labor demand for the market and locations they recruit for. Wanted Analytics uses national labor stats and national job board stats and creates real time stats that can let you know how hard it will be to recruit for a particular role, as well as the supply of that role.

X-Ray Search: A Boolean search technique of searching inside a website via search engine. The target site is usually a social media site.

Yahoo: https://www.yahoo.com/ One of the oldest search engines with name recognition. Yahoo has a loyal user base and receives traffic through its news and email services.

YouTube: https://www.youtube.com A social media site where users can post videos and people can make comments. YouTube has over one billion viewers each month so it has an enormous audience.

ZipRecruiter: https://www.ziprecruiter.com/ One of the fastest growing job boards. It works differently from most job boards as it posts your jobs to over a hundred job boards/websites.

ABOUT THE AUTHOR

Steven Mostyn, MBA, is a leading expert and innovator in recruitment and sourcing.

A bestselling author, he has written for *ERE Media/Sourcecon, Lean Human Capital, Recruiting Headlines, HealthcareSource, HR.com/Talent Acquisition Excellence Essentials,* and other forms of media. He is also frequently featured as a speaker at recruitment and sourcing seminars.

With more than 16 years of experience recruiting and sourcing for some of North America's largest companies (including Adventist Health System, Aon Hewitt, BP, BMO, IBM, Oracle, and Walmart), Steve has built successful recruiting and sourcing models in corporate, RPO, and agency . These effective models have spanned the financial services, technology, consulting, and health care industries. Steve currently works for Adventist Health System, where he manages a high-performance team of 20 sourcing specialists.

Steve earned a bachelor's degree from York University and a MBA with a focus in HR from Centenary College. In addition, he carries recruitment and HR certifications from Seneca College, HireVue, and LinkedIn.

Steve can be reached via email: steven.mostyn@yahoo.com and on social media:

https://www.linkedin.com/in/stevenmostyn
https://www.facebook.com/stevenmostynmba/
https://twitter.com/top_headhunter

CPSIA information can be obtained
at www.ICGtesting.com
Printed in the USA
LVHW020713071118
596143LV00001B/50/P